HARCOURT

Math

Practice Workbook

Grade 2

Harcourt

Orlando   Austin   Chicago   New York   Toronto   London   San Diego

Visit *The Learning Site!*
www.harcourtschool.com

CONTENTS

Understand Place Value

Circle the value of the underlined digit.

1. 6<u>5</u> (5) or 50	2. <u>3</u>7 3 or 30	3. <u>9</u>4 9 or 90
4. <u>1</u>9 1 or 10	5. 4<u>3</u> 3 or 30	6. <u>5</u>1 5 or 50
7. 8<u>7</u> 7 or 70	8. 1<u>2</u> 2 or 20	9. 7<u>5</u> 5 or 50
10. 3<u>9</u> 9 or 90	11. <u>8</u>7 8 or 80	12. <u>9</u>1 9 or 90

 Mixed Review

Solve.

13. $6 + 0 =$ _____ $6 + 4 =$ _____ $4 + 3 =$ _____

14. $5 + 1 =$ _____ $5 + 4 =$ _____ $4 + 4 =$ _____

15. $8 + 2 =$ _____ $3 + 3 =$ _____ $5 + 3 =$ _____

Read and Write Numbers to 100

Read the number.
Write the number in three different ways.

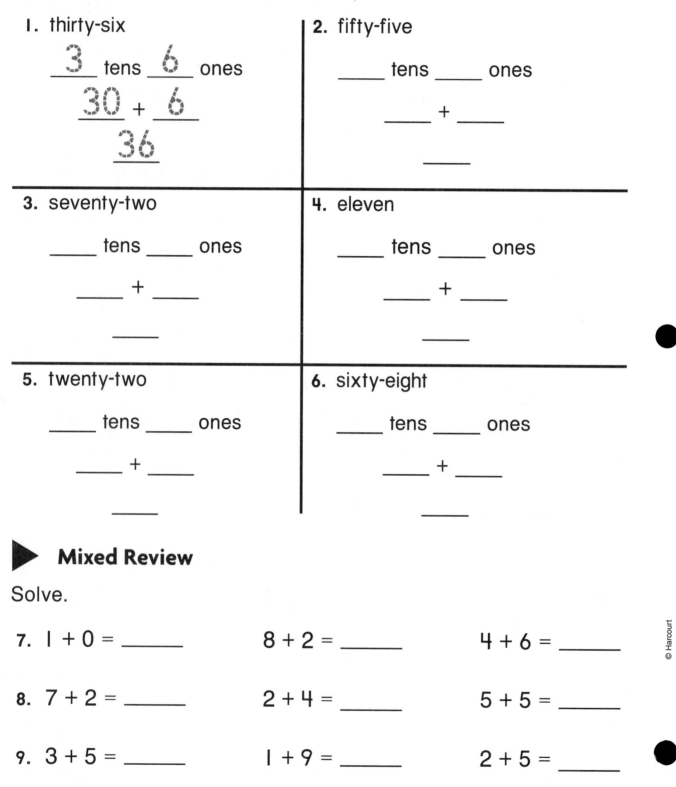

1. thirty-six

   __3__ tens __6__ ones

   __30__ + __6__

   __36__

2. fifty-five

   ____ tens ____ ones

   ____ + ____

   ____

3. seventy-two

   ____ tens ____ ones

   ____ + ____

   ____

4. eleven

   ____ tens ____ ones

   ____ + ____

   ____

5. twenty-two

   ____ tens ____ ones

   ____ + ____

   ____

6. sixty-eight

   ____ tens ____ ones

   ____ + ____

   ____

▶ **Mixed Review**

Solve.

7. $1 + 0 =$ _____ $8 + 2 =$ _____ $4 + 6 =$ _____

8. $7 + 2 =$ _____ $2 + 4 =$ _____ $5 + 5 =$ _____

9. $3 + 5 =$ _____ $1 + 9 =$ _____ $2 + 5 =$ _____

© Harcourt

Algebra: Different Ways to Show Numbers

Circle the correct ways to show each number.
Cross out and correct the other ways.

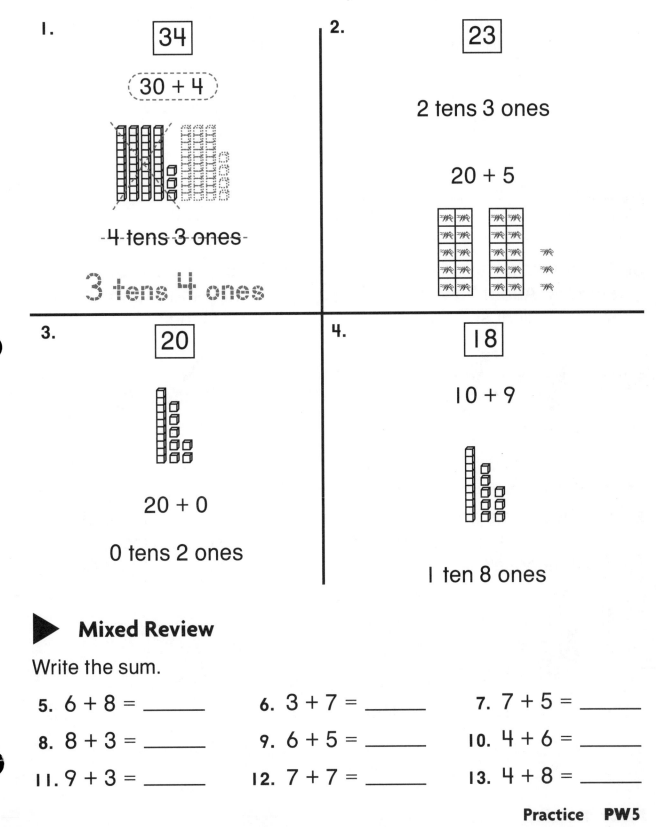

1.   34

30 + 4

4 tens 3 ones

3 tens 4 ones

2.   23

2 tens 3 ones

20 + 5

3.   20

20 + 0

0 tens 2 ones

4.   18

10 + 9

1 ten 8 ones

▶ **Mixed Review**

Write the sum.

5. 6 + 8 = _____   6. 3 + 7 = _____   7. 7 + 5 = _____

8. 8 + 3 = _____   9. 6 + 5 = _____   10. 4 + 6 = _____

11. 9 + 3 = _____   12. 7 + 7 = _____   13. 4 + 8 = _____

Problem Solving • Make Reasonable Estimates

Circle the number that makes sense.

1. Lily has a few marbles. About how many marbles might she have?

   (5)   50   100

2. Kim bought a small bag of apples. About how many apples might she have?

   10   50   100

3. Ann has a large collection of stickers. About how many stickers might she have?

   5   10   100

4. Erica bought a box of pencils. About how many pencils might be in the box?

   5   10   50

5. Nick had some balloons. About how many balloons might he have?

   5   10   100

6. Jerry took out some books from the library. About how many books might that be?

   5   50   100

Name _____

Even and Odd

Use connecting cubes. Show the number as tens and ones. Write **even** or **odd**.

1. 14 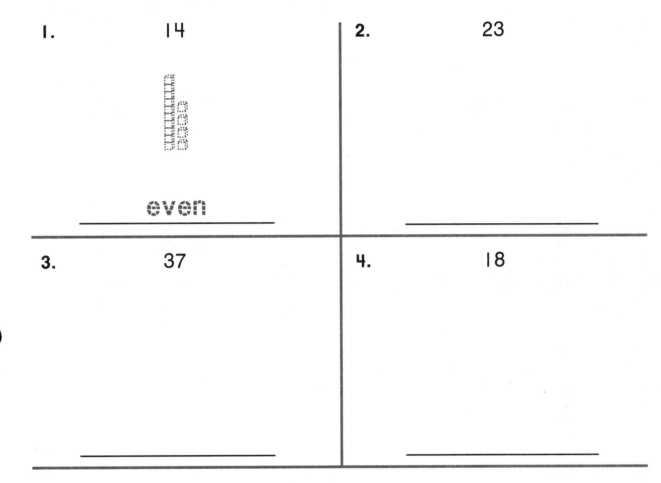 even	**2.** 23 _____
3. 37 _____	**4.** 18 _____

▶ Mixed Review

Circle the correct ways to show the number.

5. 34	3 tens 4 ones		40 + 3
6. 21	20 + 1	10 + 2	2 tens 1 one

Problem Solving • Find a Pattern

Find the pattern rule.
Complete the chart to solve.

1. How many wheels are on 6 wagons?

number of wagons	1	2	3	4	5	6
number of wheels	4	8				

Count by _____.

There are _____ wheels on 6 wagons.

---

2. How many vertices are on 7 triangles?

number of triangles	1	2	3	4	5	6	7
number of vertices							

Count by _____.

There are _____ vertices on 7 triangles.

---

3. How many fingers are on 8 hands?

number of hands	1	2	3	4	5	6	7	8
number of fingers								

Count by _____.

There are _____ fingers on 8 hands.

Name _____

Ordinal Numbers

Write the missing ordinal numbers on the boxes.
Then color the boxes that are listed.

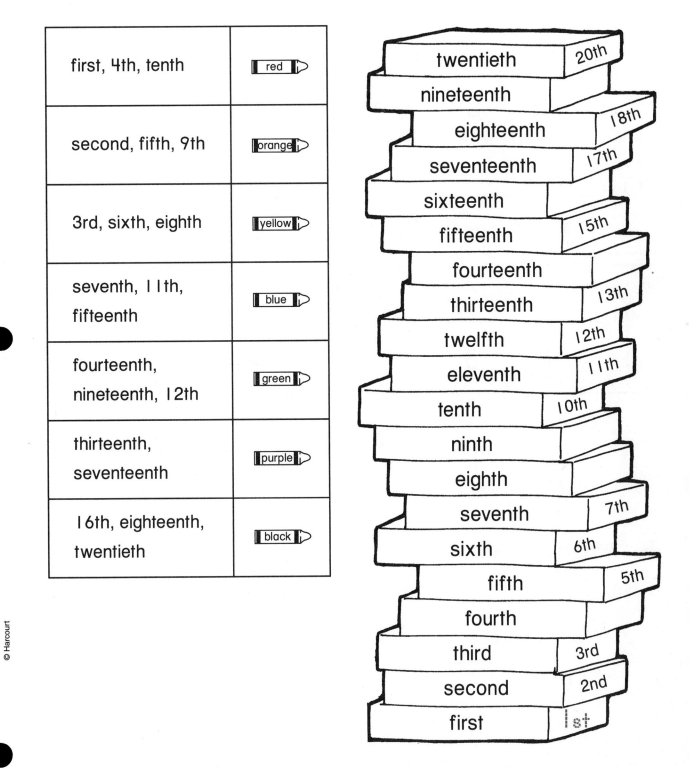

first, 4th, tenth	red
second, fifth, 9th	orange
3rd, sixth, eighth	yellow
seventh, 11th, fifteenth	blue
fourteenth, nineteenth, 12th	green
thirteenth, seventeenth	purple
16th, eighteenth, twentieth	black

twentieth 20th
nineteenth
eighteenth 18th
seventeenth 17th
sixteenth
fifteenth 15th
fourteenth
thirteenth 13th
twelfth 12th
eleventh 11th
tenth 10th
ninth
eighth
seventh 7th
sixth 6th
fifth 5th
fourth
third 3rd
second 2nd
first 1st

© Harcourt

Algebra: Compare Numbers: >, <, or =

Write greater than, less than, or equal to.
Then write >, <, or =.

1.

74 is _less than_ 89.

74 ◁ 89

2.

98 is _____ 87.

98 ○ 87

3.

48 is _____ 43.

48 ○ 43

4.

88 is _____ 99.

88 ○ 99

5.

8 is _____ 8.

8 ○ 8

6.

24 is _____ 38.

24 ○ 38

7.

19 is _____ 16.

19 ○ 16

8.

55 is _____ 55.

55 ○ 55

▶ **Mixed Review**

Solve.

9.   3 + 4 = ___   2 + 8 = ___   7 + 3 = ___

10.   9 + 0 = ___   0 + 7 = ___   5 + 3 = ___

11.   1 + 7 = ___   4 + 6 = ___   7 + 2 = ___

Order Numbers to 100

Use ⬜⬜⬜⬜⬜ ▯ or a number line. Write the missing numbers.

1. 65, 66, _67_, _____, 69, _____, _____, 72

2. 17, _____, _____, _____, 21, 22, 23, _____, _____

3. 53, 52, _____, 50, _____, _____, 47, _____, 45

4. 84, 85, _____, _____, _____, 89, _____, _____

5. _____, 31, 30, _____, _____, _____, _____, 25

6. 99, _____, _____, _____, 95, _____, _____, 92

7. 75, _____, _____, _____, 79, _____, 81, _____

▶ **Mixed Review**

Write how many ones.

8. 7 tens = ____ ones

9. 4 tens = ____ ones

10. 2 tens = ____ ones

11. 9 tens = ____ ones

12. 1 ten = ____ ones

13. 5 tens = ____ ones

10 More, 10 Less

Write the missing numbers.

1. 31, 41, __51__, 61, ____, ____, ____

2. ____, 69, 59, ____, ____, ____, ____, 9

3. 22, ____, ____, ____, 62, ____, ____, 92

4. 4, 14, ____, ____, ____, 54, ____, ____

5. ____, 75, ____, ____, 45, ____, ____, 15

6. 93, 83, ____, 63, ____, ____, 33, ____, 13

7. 18, ____, ____, ____, 58, ____, 78, ____

▶ **Mixed Review**

Write even or odd.

8. 31 _____   24 _____   8 _____

9. 17 _____   41 _____   22 _____

10. 36 _____   16 _____   29 _____

Problem Solving • Use a Model

Use the number line to solve
the problem. Round to the
nearest ten.

Think
If a number is halfway
between two tens, round to
the greater ten.

```
←—+——+——+——+——+——+——+——+——+——+——+——+——+——+——+——+——+——+——+——+——→
  40  41  42  43  44  45  46  47  48  49  50  51  52  53  54  55  56  57  58  59  60
```

1. Gail reads 43 pages in her book.
   Does Gail read about 40 or
   50 pages?   about _____ pages

2. The children make 58 paper birds.
   Do they make about 50 or 60
   paper birds?   about _____ birds

3. Joan walks for 48 minutes.
   Does she walk about 40 or
   50 minutes?   about _____ minutes

4. There are 55 apples in the box.
   Are there about 50 or 60 apples
   in the box?   about _____ apples

5. There are 52 children in the school
   play. Are there about 50 or 60
   children in the play?   about _____ children

6. There are 44 flowers in the garden.
   Are there about 40 or 50 flowers
   in the garden?   about _____ flowers

© Harcourt

Practice   PW15

Take a Survey on a Tally Table

1. Take a survey. Ask ten classmates which pet they like the best. Fill in the tally table to show their answers.

Pets We Like	
Pet	**Tally**
Cat	
Dog	
Fish	
Bird	
Hamster	

2. Which pet did the most children choose?

_____

3. Did more children like dogs or birds the best?

_____

4. How many children liked cats the best?

_____

5. Which pet did the fewest children choose?

_____

▶ **Mixed Review**

Fill in the missing numbers.

6. 21, 31, _____, _____, _____, 71, _____, _____

7. 17, _____, 37, _____, _____, _____, 77, _____

8. 86, 76, _____, _____, 46, _____, _____, _____

Use Data in Tables

Use the tally tables to answer the questions.

Favorite Sandwich for Ken's Group	
Sandwich	**Tally**
peanut butter	IIII
chicken	II
tuna	I
ham and cheese	III

Favorite Sandwich for Ken's Class	
Sandwich	**Tally**
peanut butter	⅋ℋℋ III
chicken	III
tuna	IIII
ham and cheese	⅋ℋℋ II

1. Which sandwich did the most children in the group choose as their favorite? _peanut butter_

2. Which sandwich did the most children in the class choose as their favorite? _____

3. Which sandwich did the least children in Ken's group choose? _____

4. Could the survey of the group help you predict the results for the class? _____

 **Mixed Review**

Write **even** or **odd**.

5. 21 _____   6. 30 _____   7. 12 _____

8. 32 _____   9. 6 _____   10. 24 _____

Name _____

Make a Concrete Graph

Each child has put one ball on the graph
to show what he or she likes to play.
Use the graph to answer the questions.

Sports We Like to Play		
	⚽	
	⚽	
	⚽	
🏀	⚽	⚾
🏀		
🏀	⚽	⚾
basketball	soccer	softball

Number (vertical label)

Kinds of Sports

Use the graph to answer the questions.

1. Which sport do the most children play?   _soccer_

2. How many children like to play softball?   _____

3. How many children like to play soccer?   _____

▶ Mixed Review

Read the number. Then write the number.

4. thirty-seven _____   5. sixty-five _____   6. fifteen _____

7. ninety-two _____   8. forty-six _____   9. eighty-one _____

Make a Pictograph

Use the tally table to fill in the pictograph.

Draw ☺ for every 5 children.

Children Who Ride the Bus to School	
Room Number	**Tally**
Room 201	ЖЖ
Room 202	ЖЖ ЖЖ ЖЖ ЖЖ ЖЖ
Room 203	ЖЖ ЖЖ

Children Who Ride the Bus to School										
Room 201										
Room 202										
Room 203										

Key: Each ☺ stands for 5 children.

Use the the graph to answer the questions.

1. How many children in Room 203 ride the bus to school?   10 children

2. Which room has the fewest children who ride the bus to school?   _____

3. How many more children in Room 202 ride the bus to school than in Room 203?   _____ more children

Problem Solving • Use Data from a Graph

Jamie's class made a bar graph
to show the hobbies they like.

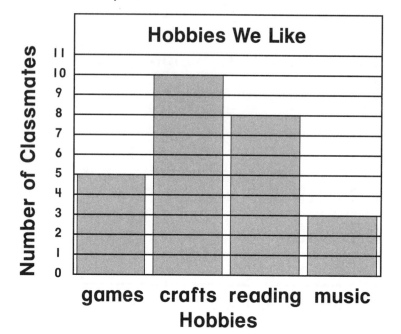

Use the bar graph to answer the questions.

1. Which hobby was chosen
   by the most children?   crafts
   _____

2. Which hobby was chosen
   by the fewest children?   _____
   _____

3. How many children like games or reading?   _____
   _____

4. How many children like crafts or music?   _____
   _____

5. How many more children
   like reading than music?   _____
   _____

6. How many more children
   like crafts than games?   _____

Count On

Circle the greater number.
Count on to find the sum.

1. (8) + 1 = __9__	2. 5 + 2 = _____	3. 3 + 10 = _____
4. 1 + 4 = _____	5. 6 + 2 = _____	6. 7 + 3 = _____
7. 3 + 8 = _____	8. 8 + 2 = _____	9. 2 + 7 = _____
10. 7 + 3 = _____	11. 1 + 5 = _____	12. 6 + 1 = _____
13. 4 + 3 = _____	14. 2 + 10 = _____	15. 3 + 6 = _____
16. 5 + 3 = _____	17. 9 + 2 = _____	18. 3 + 9 = _____

▶ **Mixed Review**

Write >, <, or =.

19. 8 ◯ 9   4 ◯ 3   5 ◯ 5

20. 10 ◯ 7   11 ◯ 9   6 ◯ 8

Doubles and Doubles Plus One

Write the sums.

1. $4 + 4 =$ _____, so $5 + 4 =$ _____

2. $5 + 5 =$ _____, so $5 + 6 =$ _____

3. $2 + 2 =$ _____, so $3 + 2 =$ _____

4. $8 + 8 =$ _____, so $8 + 9 =$ _____

5. $1 + 1 =$ _____, so $2 + 1 =$ _____

6. $7 + 7 =$ _____, so $7 + 8 =$ _____

7. $3 + 3 =$ _____, so $4 + 3 =$ _____

8. $6 + 6 =$ _____, so $6 + 7 =$ _____

9. $9 + 9 =$ _____, so $9 + 10 =$ _____

▶ **Mixed Review**

Write the sums.

10. $5 + 2 =$ _____ $1 + 4 =$ _____ $3 + 9 =$ _____

11. $7 + 1 =$ _____ $2 + 6 =$ _____ $7 + 3 =$ _____

12. $3 + 4 =$ _____ $9 + 2 =$ _____ $8 + 1 =$ _____

© Harcourt

Name _____

Make a Ten

Use a ten frame and ⚫ to find the sum.

1.
```
  7
+ 5
─────
 12
```
THINK: Start with 7. Borrow 3 from 5 to make a ten. 10 + 2 = 12

2.
```
  8
+ 6
```

3.
```
  9
+ 1
```

4.
```
  3
+ 8
```

5.
```
  5
+ 7
```

6.
```
  7
+ 4
```

7.
```
  6
+ 8
```

8.
```
  9
+ 6
```

9.
```
  7
+ 6
```

10.
```
  7
+ 7
```

11.
```
  6
+ 9
```

12.
```
  2
+ 9
```

13.
```
  5
+ 8
```

14.
```
  8
+ 4
```

15.
```
  9
+ 2
```

16.
```
  7
+ 8
```

17.
```
  3
+ 7
```

18.
```
  8
+ 2
```

19.
```
  8
+ 8
```

20.
```
  8
+ 5
```

21.
```
  8
+ 3
```

22.
```
  9
+ 9
```

23.
```
  7
+ 9
```

▶ **Mixed Review**

Circle the greater number. Count on to find the sum.

24.
```
  8
+ 2
```

25.
```
  6
+ 1
```

26.
```
  3
+ 6
```

27.
```
  1
+ 7
```

28.
```
  2
+ 8
```

© Harcourt

Name _____

Algebra: Add 3 Numbers

Write the sum.

1.

$\begin{matrix} 2 \\ 8 \\ +6 \end{matrix}$	$\begin{matrix} 10 \\ +6 \\ \hline 16 \end{matrix}$	$\begin{matrix} 2 \\ 8 \\ +6 \end{matrix}$	$\begin{matrix} 14 \\ +2 \\ \hline 16 \end{matrix}$	$\begin{matrix} 2 \\ 8 \\ +6 \end{matrix}$	$\begin{matrix} 8 \\ +8 \\ \hline 16 \end{matrix}$

2. $\begin{matrix} 3 \\ 1 \\ +3 \\ \hline \end{matrix}$ 3. $\begin{matrix} 1 \\ 6 \\ +9 \\ \hline \end{matrix}$ 4. $\begin{matrix} 5 \\ 8 \\ +2 \\ \hline \end{matrix}$ 5. $\begin{matrix} 7 \\ 5 \\ +5 \\ \hline \end{matrix}$ 6. $\begin{matrix} 2 \\ 6 \\ +4 \\ \hline \end{matrix}$ 7. $\begin{matrix} 4 \\ 3 \\ +4 \\ \hline \end{matrix}$

8. $\begin{matrix} 8 \\ 2 \\ +9 \\ \hline \end{matrix}$ 9. $\begin{matrix} 5 \\ 4 \\ +4 \\ \hline \end{matrix}$ 10. $\begin{matrix} 7 \\ 6 \\ +4 \\ \hline \end{matrix}$ 11. $\begin{matrix} 4 \\ 1 \\ +4 \\ \hline \end{matrix}$ 12. $\begin{matrix} 9 \\ 1 \\ +5 \\ \hline \end{matrix}$ 13. $\begin{matrix} 2 \\ 6 \\ +2 \\ \hline \end{matrix}$

14. $\begin{matrix} 3 \\ 4 \\ +1 \\ \hline \end{matrix}$ 15. $\begin{matrix} 7 \\ 3 \\ +4 \\ \hline \end{matrix}$ 16. $\begin{matrix} 9 \\ 0 \\ +9 \\ \hline \end{matrix}$ 17. $\begin{matrix} 2 \\ 4 \\ +6 \\ \hline \end{matrix}$ 18. $\begin{matrix} 8 \\ 3 \\ +2 \\ \hline \end{matrix}$ 19. $\begin{matrix} 9 \\ 5 \\ +2 \\ \hline \end{matrix}$

► **Mixed Review**

Write the sum.

20. $7 + 1 =$ _____ $2 + 8 =$ _____ $9 + 3 =$ _____

21. $4 + 4 =$ _____ $7 + 7 =$ _____ $3 + 3 =$ _____

22. $5 + 6 =$ _____ $8 + 9 =$ _____ $9 + 10 =$ _____

Problem Solving • Draw a Picture

Draw a picture to solve. Write the number sentence.

1. 9 brown bears and 7 black bears played. How many bears in all played?

   9 (+) 7 (=) 16 bears

2. 7 cats sat on the porch. Then 8 more cats joined them. How many cats were on the porch?

   ___ ◯ ___ ◯ ___ cats

3. 6 yellow fish and 8 orange fish swam in a fish tank. How many fish swam in the tank?

   ___ ◯ ___ ◯ ___ fish

4. There were 7 children in the yard and 3 children in the house. How many children were there in all?

   ___ ◯ ___ ◯ ___ children

Count Back

Count back to find the difference.

1. $8 - 1 = \underline{7}$ $4 - 2 = \underline{}$ $6 - 1 = \underline{}$

2. $5 - 2 = \underline{}$ $9 - 3 = \underline{}$ $10 - 2 = \underline{}$

3. $\begin{array}{r} 7 \\ -3 \\ \hline \end{array}$ $\begin{array}{r} 5 \\ -1 \\ \hline \end{array}$ $\begin{array}{r} 8 \\ -3 \\ \hline \end{array}$ $\begin{array}{r} 4 \\ -1 \\ \hline \end{array}$ $\begin{array}{r} 6 \\ -2 \\ \hline \end{array}$

4. $\begin{array}{r} 10 \\ -3 \\ \hline \end{array}$ $\begin{array}{r} 9 \\ -2 \\ \hline \end{array}$ $\begin{array}{r} 11 \\ -2 \\ \hline \end{array}$ $\begin{array}{r} 7 \\ -2 \\ \hline \end{array}$ $\begin{array}{r} 3 \\ -2 \\ \hline \end{array}$

5. $\begin{array}{r} 8 \\ -2 \\ \hline \end{array}$ $\begin{array}{r} 3 \\ -1 \\ \hline \end{array}$ $\begin{array}{r} 9 \\ -1 \\ \hline \end{array}$ $\begin{array}{r} 12 \\ -1 \\ \hline \end{array}$ $\begin{array}{r} 7 \\ -1 \\ \hline \end{array}$

6. $\begin{array}{r} 3 \\ -2 \\ \hline \end{array}$ $\begin{array}{r} 10 \\ -1 \\ \hline \end{array}$ $\begin{array}{r} 6 \\ -3 \\ \hline \end{array}$ $\begin{array}{r} 11 \\ -3 \\ \hline \end{array}$ $\begin{array}{r} 5 \\ -3 \\ \hline \end{array}$

▶ **Mixed Review**

Write the missing numbers.

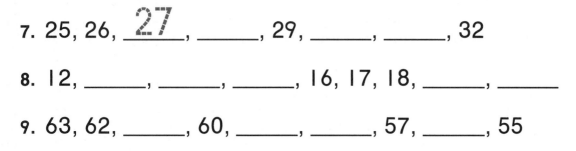

7. 25, 26, __27__, _____, 29, _____, _____, 32

8. 12, _____, _____, _____, 16, 17, 18, _____, _____

9. 63, 62, _____, 60, _____, _____, 57, _____, 55

Algebra: Fact Families

Complete the fact families.

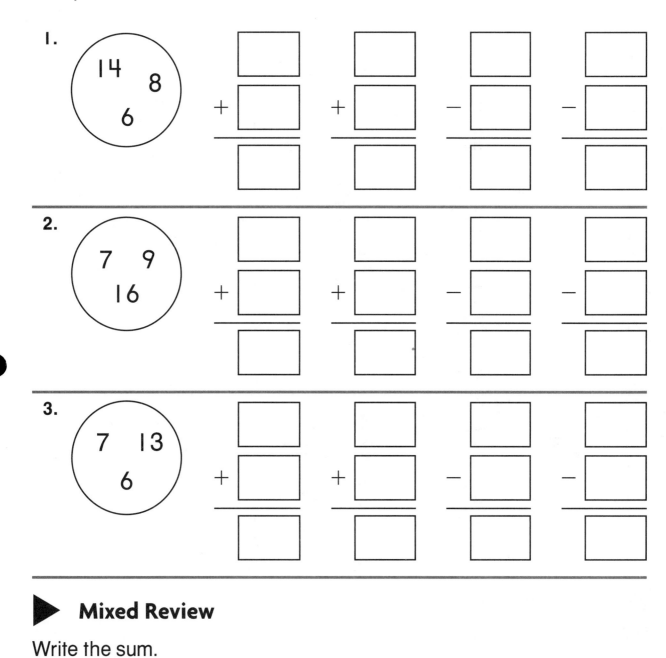

1.

14 8
6

☐ + ☐ = ☐   ☐ + ☐ = ☐   ☐ − ☐ = ☐   ☐ − ☐ = ☐

2.

7 9
16

☐ + ☐ = ☐   ☐ + ☐ = ☐   ☐ − ☐ = ☐   ☐ − ☐ = ☐

3.

7 13
6

☐ + ☐ = ☐   ☐ + ☐ = ☐   ☐ − ☐ = ☐   ☐ − ☐ = ☐

▶ **Mixed Review**

Write the sum.

4. $6 + 7 =$ _____ $5 + 6 =$ _____ $8 + 9 =$ _____

5. $3 + 4 =$ _____ $7 + 8 =$ _____ $4 + 5 =$ _____

Relate Addition to Subtraction

Find the difference.
Write the addition fact to help you.

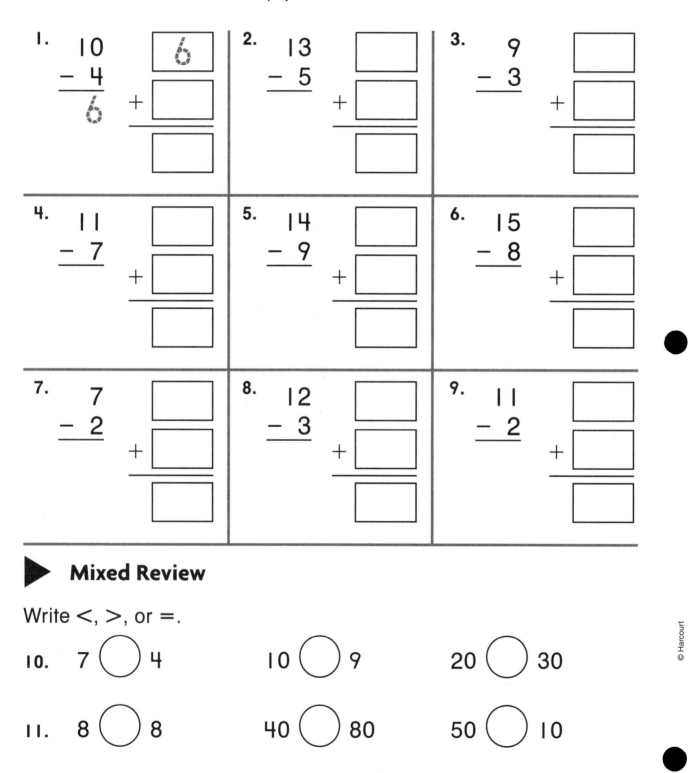

1.
$$\begin{array}{r} 10 \\ -\ 4 \\ \hline 6 \end{array}$$
6
+ ☐
☐

2.
$$\begin{array}{r} 13 \\ -\ 5 \\ \hline \end{array}$$
☐
+ ☐
☐

3.
$$\begin{array}{r} 9 \\ -\ 3 \\ \hline \end{array}$$
☐
+ ☐
☐

4.
$$\begin{array}{r} 11 \\ -\ 7 \\ \hline \end{array}$$
☐
+ ☐
☐

5.
$$\begin{array}{r} 14 \\ -\ 9 \\ \hline \end{array}$$
☐
+ ☐
☐

6.
$$\begin{array}{r} 15 \\ -\ 8 \\ \hline \end{array}$$
☐
+ ☐
☐

7.
$$\begin{array}{r} 7 \\ -\ 2 \\ \hline \end{array}$$
☐
+ ☐
☐

8.
$$\begin{array}{r} 12 \\ -\ 3 \\ \hline \end{array}$$
☐
+ ☐
☐

9.
$$\begin{array}{r} 11 \\ -\ 2 \\ \hline \end{array}$$
☐
+ ☐
☐

▶ **Mixed Review**

Write <, >, or =.

10.   7 ◯ 4   10 ◯ 9   20 ◯ 30

11.   8 ◯ 8   40 ◯ 80   50 ◯ 10

Algebra: Missing Addends

Use addition and a related fact to find the missing addend.

1. $6 + \underline{8} = 14$ $\qquad$ $14 - 6 = \underline{8}$

2. $\underline{} + 5 = 12$ $\qquad$ $12 - 5 = \underline{}$

3. $9 + \underline{} = 13$ $\qquad$ $13 - 9 = \underline{}$

4. $8 + \underline{} = 16$ $\qquad$ $16 - 8 = \underline{}$

5. $\underline{} + 6 = 13$ $\qquad$ $13 - 6 = \underline{}$

6. $\underline{} + 9 = 18$ $\qquad$ $18 - 9 = \underline{}$

7. $8 + \underline{} = 10$ $\qquad$ $10 - 8 = \underline{}$

8. $9 + \underline{} = 15$ $\qquad$ $15 - 9 = \underline{}$

▶ **Mixed Review**

Write the sum or difference.

9. $6 + 6 = \underline{}$ $\qquad$ $8 + 5 = \underline{}$ $\qquad$ $3 + 7 = \underline{}$

10. $8 - 3 = \underline{}$ $\qquad$ $9 - 2 = \underline{}$ $\qquad$ $4 + 6 = \underline{}$

11. $7 - 7 = \underline{}$ $\qquad$ $7 + 5 = \underline{}$ $\qquad$ $9 - 8 = \underline{}$

Algebra: Names for Numbers

Write an addition and a subtraction name for each number.

1. | 6 | 3 + 3   9 – 3

2. | 15 | ____ + ____   ____ – ____

3. | 4 | ____ + ____   ____ – ____

4. | 16 | ____ + ____   ____ – ____

5. | 7 | ____ + ____   ____ – ____

6. | 13 | ____ + ____   ____ – ____

7. | 18 | ____ + ____   ____ – ____

8. | 5 | ____ + ____   ____ – ____

▶ **Mixed Review**

Write even or odd.

9. 12 _____   8 _____   27 _____

10. 33 _____   40 _____   15 _____

Problem Solving • Write a Number Sentence

Draw a picture or make a model.
Write a number sentence to solve.

1. Julie buys 13 apples. 5 of them are red and the rest are green. How many green apples does Julie buy.

    13 ⊖ 5 ⊜ 8

    green apples

2. Mary has 6 dolls. Tasha has 4 dolls. How many more dolls does Mary have than Tasha?

    ___ ◯ ___ ◯ ___

    more dolls

3. Joel plants 7 carrot seeds. He also plants some flower seeds. He plants 13 seeds altogether. How many flower seeds does Joel plant?

    ___ ◯ ___ ◯ ___

    flower seeds

4. Eddie has 16 oranges. He gives 8 of them away. How many oranges does Eddie have left?

    ___ ◯ ___ ◯ ___

    oranges left

Mental Math: Add Tens

Add.

1. I ten + 2 tens = **3** tens

   $\underline{10} + \underline{20} = \underline{30}$

2. 3 tens + 2 tens = ___ tens

   ____ + ____ = ____

3. 3 tens + 3 tens = ___ tens

   ____ + ____ = ____

4. 0 tens + 2 tens = ___ tens

   ____ + ____ = ____

5. 4 tens + 3 tens = ___ tens

   ____ + ____ = ____

6. I ten + 3 tens = ___ tens

   ____ + ____ = ____

7. 4 tens + 4 tens = ___ tens

   ____ + ____ = ____

8. 6 ten + 3 tens = ___ tens

   ____ + ____ = ____

▶ **Mixed Review**

Write <, >, or =.

9. 3 ◯ 10 | 2 ◯ 2 | 16 ◯ 10 | 36 ◯ 24

10. 78 ◯ 78 | 50 ◯ 53 | 14 ◯ 18 | 68 ◯ 65

Mental Math: Count on Tens and Ones

Count on to add.

1.
30	75	61	54	18
+39	+ 3	+30	+ 2	+20
69				

2.
1	44	67	83	2
+29	+20	+10	+ 3	+41

3.
90	3	54	74	38
+ 3	+18	+30	+ 2	+10

4.
2	21	36	55	67
+59	+ 3	+20	+10	+ 2

▶ **Mixed Review**

What comes next? Write the number.

5. 3, 6, 9, ——   7, 8, 9, ——   22, 24, 26, ——

6. 25, 30, 35, ——   20, 30, 40, ——   10, 12, 14, ——

Regroup Ones as Tens

Use Workmat 3 and ▭▭▭ ▯ .

	Show.	Add.	Do you need to regroup? Circle Yes or No.	How many tens and ones?
1.	16	7	(Yes) No	__2__ tens __3__ ones
2.	34	7	Yes No	____ tens ____ ones
3.	46	4	Yes No	____ tens ____ ones
4.	63	5	Yes No	____ tens ____ ones
5.	38	5	Yes No	____ tens ____ ones

▶ **Mixed Review**

Write the difference.

6. $13 - 7 =$ _____   7. $10 - 10 =$ _____   8. $14 - 7 =$ _____

9. $15 - 8 =$ _____   10. $16 - 8 =$ _____   11. $12 - 5 =$ _____

Name _____

Model 2-Digit Addition

Use Workmat 3 and ▭▭▭▭▭▭ ▯.
Draw the regrouping if you need to. Then add.

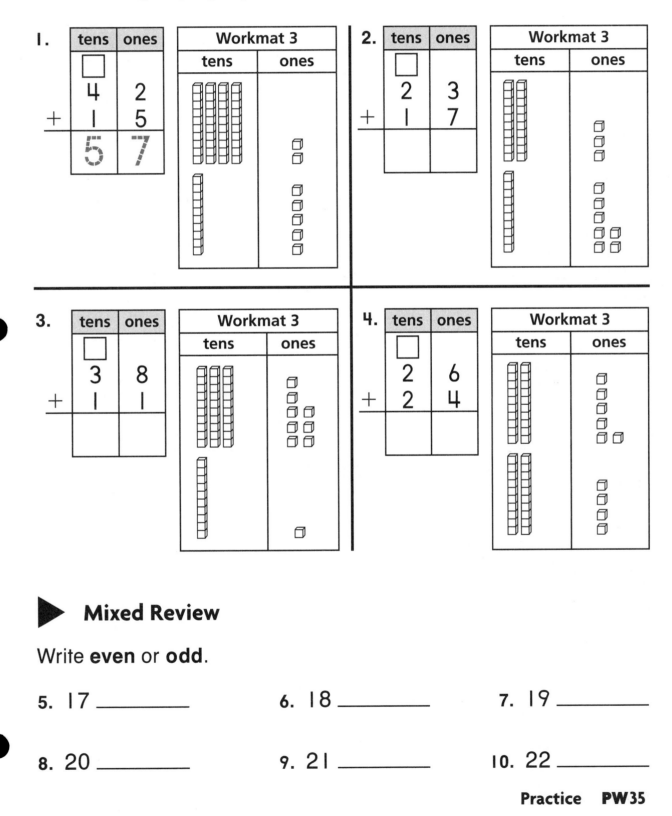

1.

tens	ones
☐	
4	2
+ 1	5
5	7

2.

tens	ones
☐	
2	3
+ 1	7

3.

tens	ones
☐	
3	8
+ 1	1

4.

tens	ones
☐	
2	6
+ 2	4

▶ **Mixed Review**

Write **even** or **odd**.

5. 17 _____

6. 18 _____

7. 19 _____

8. 20 _____

9. 21 _____

10. 22 _____

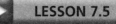

Problem Solving • Make a Model

Use Workmat 3 and ⬚⬚⬚⬚⬚⬚⬚ ▢.
Add. Regroup if you need to.
Write the sum.

1. The sports store sold 13 mitts last week and 17 mitts this week. How many mitts were sold?

   _30_ mitts

tens	ones
1	3
+ 1	7
3	0

2. There are 20 baseball bats for sale on the shelf. There are 19 bats in the back room. How many bats are for sale in all?

   ____ bats

tens	ones
+	

3. One box holds 18 baseballs. Another box holds 23 baseballs. How many baseballs are there in all?

   ____ baseballs

tens	ones
+	

4. 19 children bought baseball caps on Monday. 16 children bought caps on Tuesday. How many caps were sold in all?

   ____ caps

tens	ones
+	

© Harcourt

Add 1-Digit Numbers

Use Workmat 3 and ⬚⬚⬚⬚⬚⬚⬚⬚ ▢ . Add.

THINK Do I need to regroup 10 ones as 1 ten?

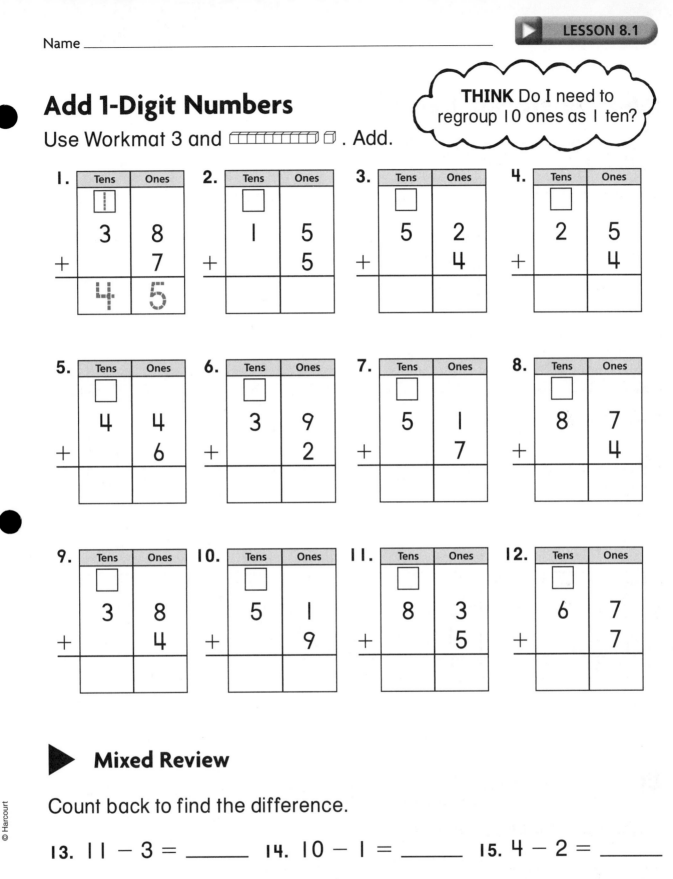

1.
Tens	Ones
⬚	
3	8
+	7
4	5

2.
Tens	Ones
⬚	
1	5
+	5

3.
Tens	Ones
⬚	
5	2
+	4

4.
Tens	Ones
⬚	
2	5
+	4

5.
Tens	Ones
⬚	
4	4
+	6

6.
Tens	Ones
⬚	
3	9
+	2

7.
Tens	Ones
⬚	
5	1
+	7

8.
Tens	Ones
⬚	
8	7
+	4

9.
Tens	Ones
⬚	
3	8
+	4

10.
Tens	Ones
⬚	
5	1
+	9

11.
Tens	Ones
⬚	
8	3
+	5

12.
Tens	Ones
⬚	
6	7
+	7

▶ **Mixed Review**

Count back to find the difference.

13. $11 - 3 =$ _____   14. $10 - 1 =$ _____   15. $4 - 2 =$ _____

16. $6 - 1 =$ _____   17. $12 - 3 =$ _____   18. $7 - 1 =$ _____

Add 2-Digit Numbers

Use Workmat 3 and ⌷⌷⌷⌷⌷⌷⌷ ▱ .
Add. Regroup if you need to.

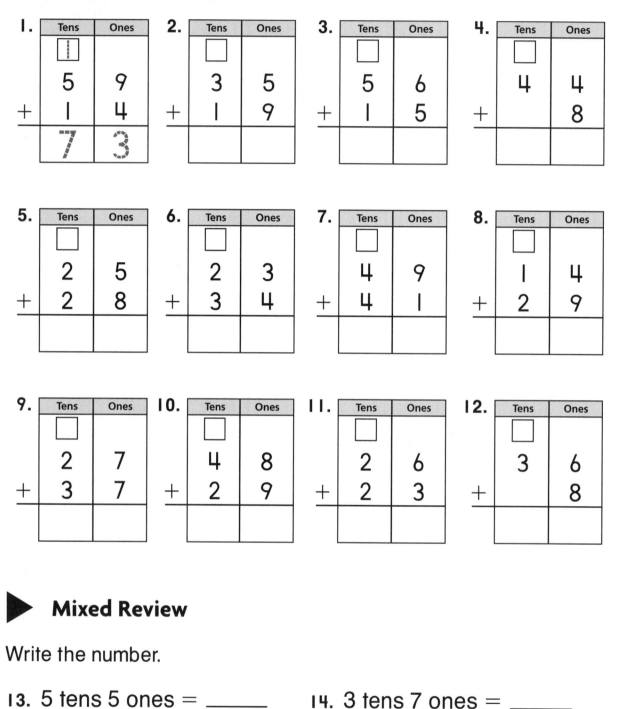

1.

Tens	Ones
▯	
5	9
+ 1	4
7	3

2.

Tens	Ones
▢	
3	5
+ 1	9

3.

Tens	Ones
▢	
5	6
+ 1	5

4.

Tens	Ones
▢	
4	4
+	8

5.

Tens	Ones
▢	
2	5
+ 2	8

6.

Tens	Ones
▢	
2	3
+ 3	4

7.

Tens	Ones
▢	
4	9
+ 4	1

8.

Tens	Ones
▢	
1	4
+ 2	9

9.

Tens	Ones
▢	
2	7
+ 3	7

10.

Tens	Ones
▢	
4	8
+ 2	9

11.

Tens	Ones
▢	
2	6
+ 2	3

12.

Tens	Ones
▢	
3	6
+	8

▶ **Mixed Review**

Write the number.

13. 5 tens 5 ones = _____   14. 3 tens 7 ones = _____

15. 6 tens 3 ones = _____   16. 4 tens 5 ones = _____

© Harcourt

More 2-Digit Addition

Add. Regroup if you need to.

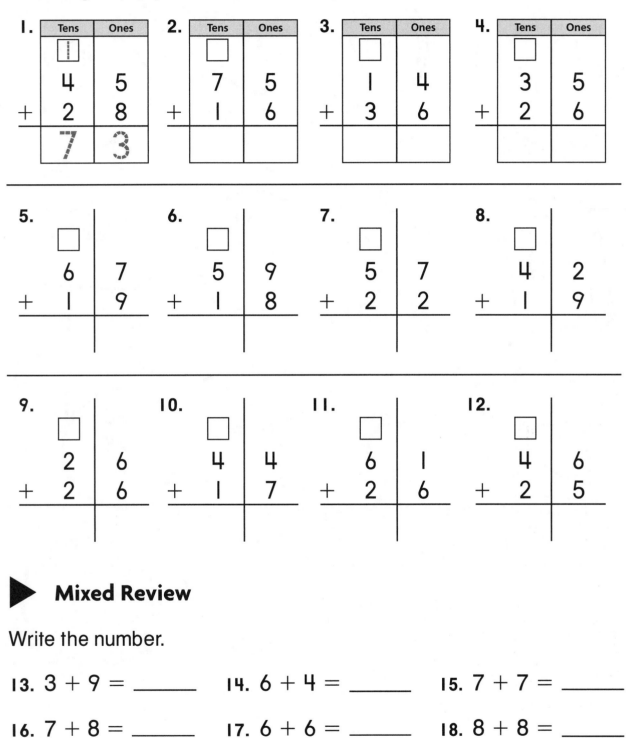

1.

Tens	Ones
[1]	
4	5
+ 2	8
7	3

2.

Tens	Ones
[ ]	
7	5
+ 1	6

3.

Tens	Ones
[ ]	
1	4
+ 3	6

4.

Tens	Ones
[ ]	
3	5
+ 2	6

5.

[ ]	
6	7
+ 1	9

6.

[ ]	
5	9
+ 1	8

7.

[ ]	
5	7
+ 2	2

8.

[ ]	
4	2
+ 1	9

9.

[ ]	
2	6
+ 2	6

10.

[ ]	
4	4
+ 1	7

11.

[ ]	
6	1
+ 2	6

12.

[ ]	
4	6
+ 2	5

▶ **Mixed Review**

Write the number.

13. $3 + 9 =$ _____   **14.** $6 + 4 =$ _____   **15.** $7 + 7 =$ _____

16. $7 + 8 =$ _____   **17.** $6 + 6 =$ _____   **18.** $8 + 8 =$ _____

19. $8 + 9 =$ _____   **20.** $6 + 5 =$ _____

Name _____

Practice 2-Digit Addition

Add.

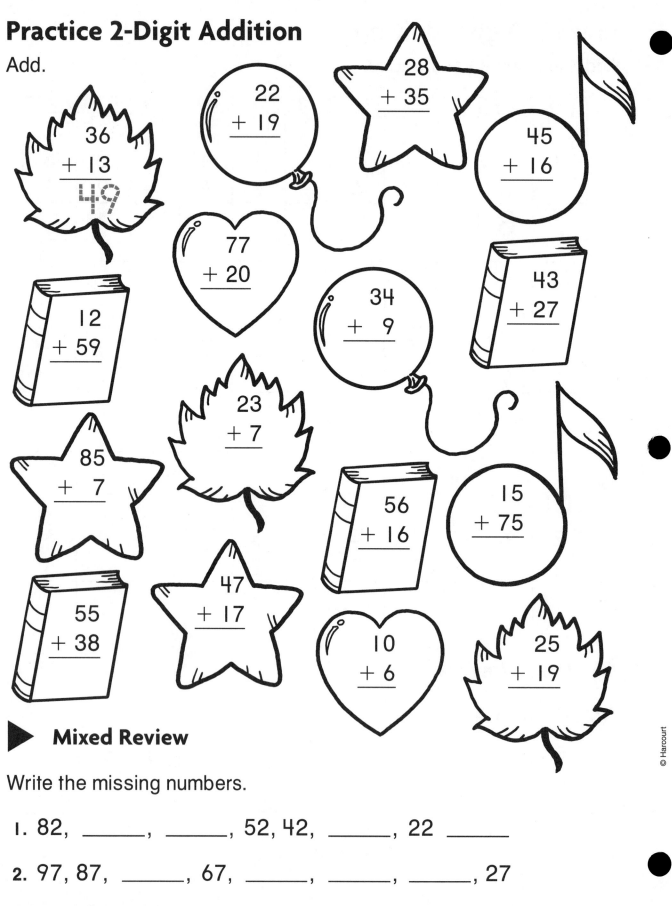

$$\begin{array}{r} 36 \\ + 13 \\ \hline 49 \end{array}$$

$$\begin{array}{r} 22 \\ + 19 \\ \hline \end{array}$$

$$\begin{array}{r} 28 \\ + 35 \\ \hline \end{array}$$

$$\begin{array}{r} 45 \\ + 16 \\ \hline \end{array}$$

$$\begin{array}{r} 77 \\ + 20 \\ \hline \end{array}$$

$$\begin{array}{r} 12 \\ + 59 \\ \hline \end{array}$$

$$\begin{array}{r} 34 \\ + 9 \\ \hline \end{array}$$

$$\begin{array}{r} 43 \\ + 27 \\ \hline \end{array}$$

$$\begin{array}{r} 23 \\ + 7 \\ \hline \end{array}$$

$$\begin{array}{r} 85 \\ + 7 \\ \hline \end{array}$$

$$\begin{array}{r} 56 \\ + 16 \\ \hline \end{array}$$

$$\begin{array}{r} 15 \\ + 75 \\ \hline \end{array}$$

$$\begin{array}{r} 55 \\ + 38 \\ \hline \end{array}$$

$$\begin{array}{r} 47 \\ + 17 \\ \hline \end{array}$$

$$\begin{array}{r} 10 \\ + 6 \\ \hline \end{array}$$

$$\begin{array}{r} 25 \\ + 19 \\ \hline \end{array}$$

▶ Mixed Review

Write the missing numbers.

1. 82, _____, _____, 52, 42, _____, 22 _____

2. 97, 87, _____, 67, _____, _____, _____, 27

Rewrite 2-Digit Addition

Rewrite the numbers in each problem.
Then add.

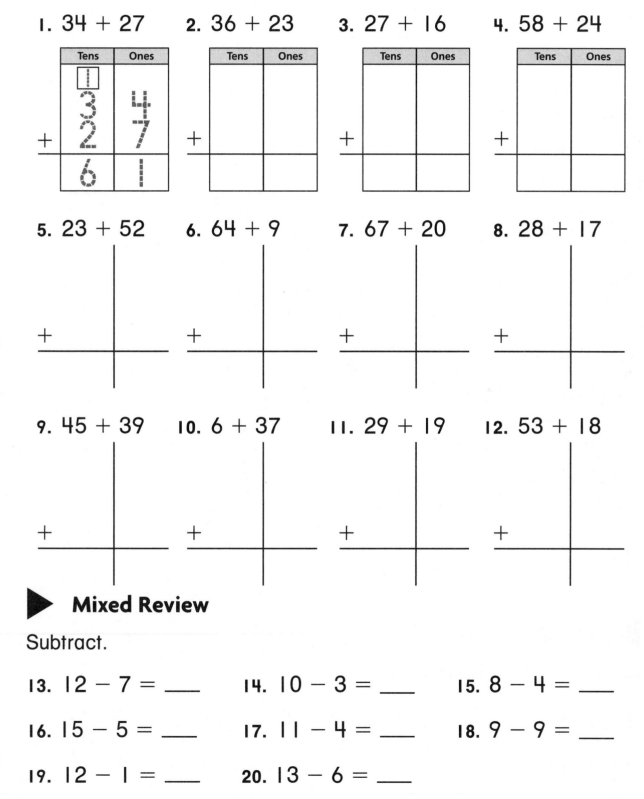

1. 34 + 27

Tens	Ones
☐1	
3	4
+ 2	7
6	1

2. 36 + 23

Tens	Ones
+	

3. 27 + 16

Tens	Ones
+	

4. 58 + 24

Tens	Ones
+	

5. 23 + 52

6. 64 + 9

7. 67 + 20

8. 28 + 17

9. 45 + 39

10. 6 + 37

11. 29 + 19

12. 53 + 18

▶ **Mixed Review**

Subtract.

13. $12 - 7 =$ ___   14. $10 - 3 =$ ___   15. $8 - 4 =$ ___

16. $15 - 5 =$ ___   17. $11 - 4 =$ ___   18. $9 - 9 =$ ___

19. $12 - 1 =$ ___   20. $13 - 6 =$ ___

Estimate Sums

Use the number line to round
each number to the nearest ten.
Estimate the sum.

THINK: If a number is
halfway between two tens,
round to the greater ten.

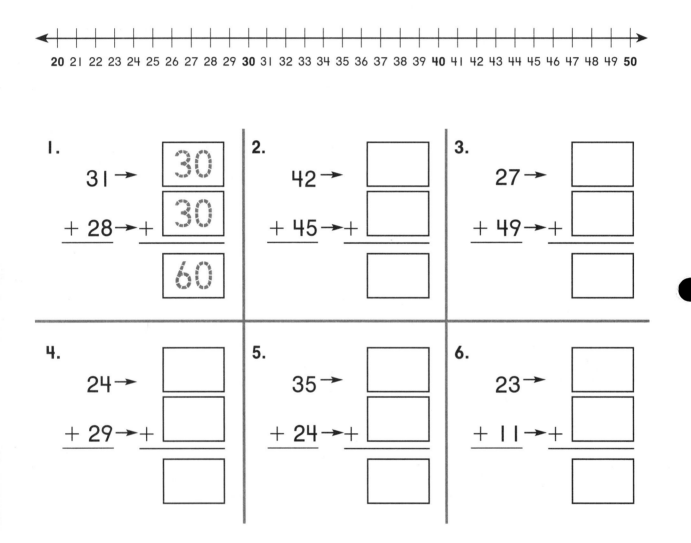

20 21 22 23 24 25 26 27 28 29 **30** 31 32 33 34 35 36 37 38 39 **40** 41 42 43 44 45 46 47 48 49 **50**

1.

$31 \rightarrow$ [30]

$+ 28 \rightarrow +$ [30]

[60]

2.

$42 \rightarrow$ ☐

$+ 45 \rightarrow +$ ☐

☐

3.

$27 \rightarrow$ ☐

$+ 49 \rightarrow +$ ☐

☐

4.

$24 \rightarrow$ ☐

$+ 29 \rightarrow +$ ☐

☐

5.

$35 \rightarrow$ ☐

$+ 24 \rightarrow +$ ☐

☐

6.

$23 \rightarrow$ ☐

$+ 11 \rightarrow +$ ☐

☐

▶ **Mixed Review**

Circle the names for each number.

7. 11	$4 + 7$	$12 - 1$	$5 + 5$	$8 + 3$	$15 - 2$
8. 12	$14 - 1$	$4 + 8$	$9 + 3$	$15 - 3$	$12 + 0$

© Harcourt

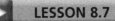

Problem Solving • Too Much Information

Draw a line through any information you do not need. Then solve.

> **THINK:** Is there any information I do not need?

1. Hal swam 42 laps on Monday and 39 laps on Tuesday. ~~He swam the butterfly stroke for 7 laps.~~ How many laps did Hal swim on Monday and Tuesday?

   __81__ laps

$$\begin{array}{r} 42 \\ + 39 \\ \hline 81 \end{array}$$

2. Last week Mrs. Jones baked 25 loaves of rye bread and 38 loaves of wheat bread. She also baked 17 muffins. How many loaves of bread did Mrs. Jones bake?

   _____ loaves

3. There are 17 cars parked on one side of the street. There are 21 cars parked on the other side. How many cars are parked on the street?

   _____ cars

4. Tyrone put 17 pennies into his right pocket. He put 23 pennies into his left pocket. He still had 4 pennies on his desk. How many pennies did Tyrone put into his pockets?

   _____ pennies

© Harcourt

Mental Math: Subtract Tens

Subtract. Write the missing numbers.

1. 3 tens
    − 2 tens
    ‾‾‾‾‾‾‾
    1 ten

    30
    − 20
    ‾‾‾‾
    10

2. 8 tens
    − 4 tens
    ‾‾‾‾‾‾‾
    tens

    [ ]
    − [ ]
    ‾‾‾‾
    [ ]

3. 9 tens
    − 7 tens
    ‾‾‾‾‾‾‾
    tens

    [ ]
    − [ ]
    ‾‾‾‾
    [ ]

4. 6 tens
    − 1 ten
    ‾‾‾‾‾‾
    tens

    [ ]
    − [ ]
    ‾‾‾‾
    [ ]

5. 5 tens
    − 0 tens
    ‾‾‾‾‾‾‾
    tens

    [ ]
    − [ ]
    ‾‾‾‾
    [ ]

6. 7 tens
    − 2 tens
    ‾‾‾‾‾‾‾
    tens

    [ ]
    − [ ]
    ‾‾‾‾
    [ ]

▶ **Mixed Review**

Add.

7.
35	24	19	48
+ 54	+ 17	+ 19	+ 24

8.
62	28	54	47
+ 29	+ 12	+ 27	+ 32

Mental Math: Count Back Tens and Ones

Count back to subtract.

1. $\begin{array}{r} 66 \\ -\ 20 \\ \hline 46 \end{array}$	$\begin{array}{r} 52 \\ -\ 40 \\ \hline \end{array}$	$\begin{array}{r} 77 \\ -\ 3 \\ \hline \end{array}$	$\begin{array}{r} 22 \\ -\ 10 \\ \hline \end{array}$
2. $\begin{array}{r} 48 \\ -\ 3 \\ \hline \end{array}$	$\begin{array}{r} 65 \\ -\ 30 \\ \hline \end{array}$	$\begin{array}{r} 89 \\ -\ 70 \\ \hline \end{array}$	$\begin{array}{r} 99 \\ -\ 2 \\ \hline \end{array}$
3. $\begin{array}{r} 36 \\ -\ 3 \\ \hline \end{array}$	$\begin{array}{r} 44 \\ -\ 20 \\ \hline \end{array}$	$\begin{array}{r} 18 \\ -\ 3 \\ \hline \end{array}$	$\begin{array}{r} 59 \\ -\ 10 \\ \hline \end{array}$
4. $\begin{array}{r} 35 \\ -\ 2 \\ \hline \end{array}$	$\begin{array}{r} 78 \\ -\ 30 \\ \hline \end{array}$	$\begin{array}{r} 42 \\ -\ 10 \\ \hline \end{array}$	$\begin{array}{r} 87 \\ -\ 1 \\ \hline \end{array}$

▶ Mixed Review

Solve.

5. $15 - 10 =$ _____ $\qquad$ $12 - 8 =$ _____ $\qquad$ $16 - 13 =$ _____

6. $11 - 7 =$ _____ $\qquad$ $12 - 6 =$ _____ $\qquad$ $15 - 8 =$ _____

7. $17 - 5 =$ _____ $\qquad$ $15 - 13 =$ _____ $\qquad$ $14 - 11 =$ _____

8. $16 - 9 =$ _____ $\qquad$ $14 - 7 =$ _____ $\qquad$ $13 - 10 =$ _____

Regroup Tens as Ones

Use Workmat 3 and .

	Show.	Subtract.	Do you need to regroup? Circle Yes or No.	How many tens and ones are left?
1.	24	8	(Yes) No	__1__ tens __6__ ones
2.	32	5	Yes No	_____ tens _____ ones
3.	23	9	Yes No	_____ tens _____ ones
4.	70	8	Yes No	_____ tens _____ ones
5.	55	2	Yes No	_____ tens _____ ones

▶ **Mixed Review**

Add.

6. $7 + 6 =$ _____   7. $9 + 2 =$ _____   8. $8 + 6 =$ _____

9. $8 + 8 =$ _____   10. $4 + 8 =$ _____   11. $9 + 5 =$ _____

12. $5 + 7 =$ _____   13. $11 + 5 =$ _____   14. $3 + 7 =$ _____

© Harcourt

Name _____

Model 2-Digit Subtraction

Use Workmat 3 and 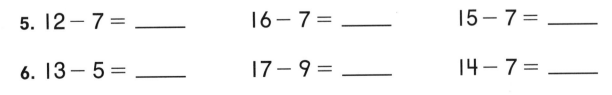 . Draw the regrouping.
Then subtract.

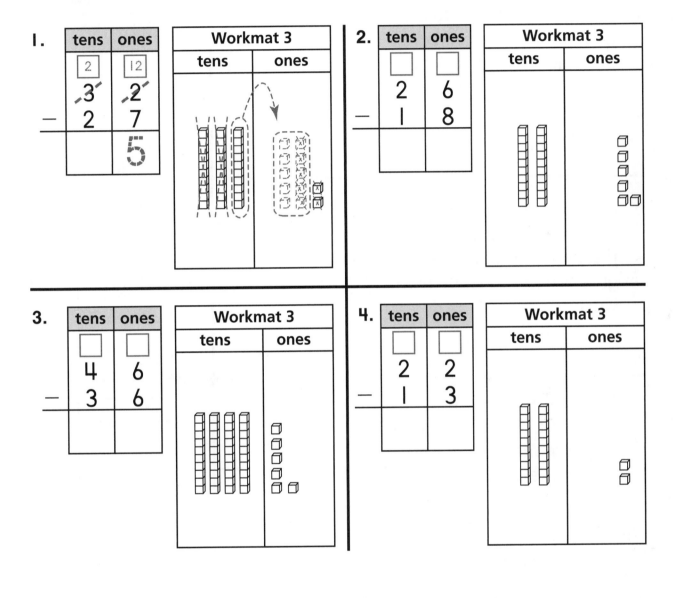

1.

tens	ones
2̷ 3	1̷2 2
− 2	7
	5

Workmat 3

tens	ones

2.

tens	ones
☐ 2	☐ 6
− 1	8

Workmat 3

tens	ones

3.

tens	ones
☐ 4	☐ 6
− 3	6

Workmat 3

tens	ones

4.

tens	ones
☐ 2	☐ 2
− 1	3

Workmat 3

tens	ones

▶ **Mixed Review**

Subtract.

5. $12 - 7 =$ _____ $16 - 7 =$ _____ $15 - 7 =$ _____

6. $13 - 5 =$ _____ $17 - 9 =$ _____ $14 - 7 =$ _____

Problem Solving • Choose the Operation

Use Workmat 3 and ⬚⬚⬚⬚⬚⬚⬚ ⬚.
Add or subtract. Write the sum or difference.

1. Josh put 12 toy cars on a
shelf and 12 toy cars in a
box. How many toy cars
does he have in all?

   __24__ toy cars

	tens	ones
+	1	2
	1	2
	2	4

2. Cara is skating with 24 girls.
Then her mom drives 5 of
the girls home. How many
girls are left to skate with
Cara?

   _____ girls

	tens	ones
○	☐	☐

3. There are 16 toy train cars on
the track. Then 4 of them fall
off. How many train cars are
left on the track?

   _____ train cars

	tens	ones
○	☐	☐

4. Jack got 16 rubber dinosaurs
for his birthday. He already
had 15 dinosaurs. How many
rubber dinosaurs does he
have now?

   _____ dinosaurs

	tens	ones
○	☐	

Subtract 1-Digit Numbers

Use Workmat 3 and 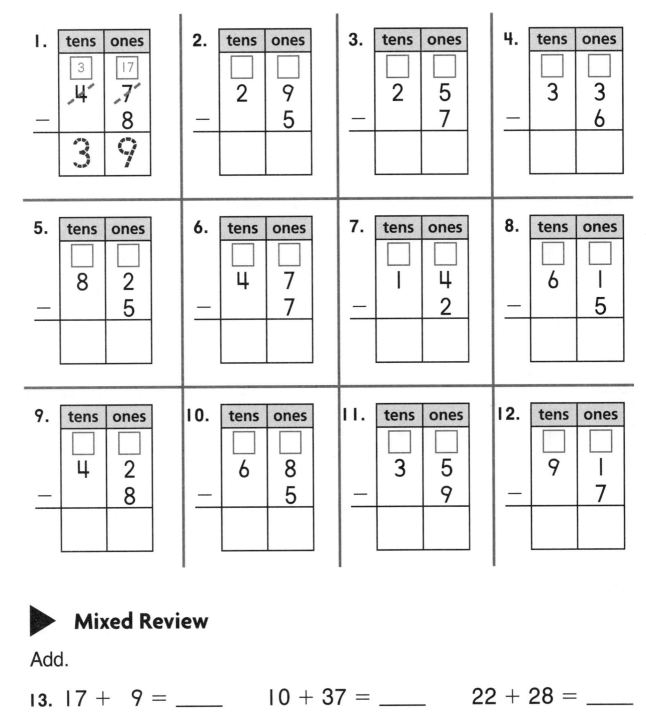 . Subtract.

1.

tens	ones
3̶ 4	1̶7̶ 7̶
−	8
3	9

2.

tens	ones
☐	☐
2	9
−	5

3.

tens	ones
☐	☐
2	5
−	7

4.

tens	ones
☐	☐
3	3
−	6

5.

tens	ones
☐	☐
8	2
−	5

6.

tens	ones
☐	☐
4	7
−	7

7.

tens	ones
☐	☐
1	4
−	2

8.

tens	ones
☐	☐
6	1
−	5

9.

tens	ones
☐	☐
4	2
−	8

10.

tens	ones
☐	☐
6	8
−	5

11.

tens	ones
☐	☐
3	5
−	9

12.

tens	ones
☐	☐
9	1
−	7

▶ **Mixed Review**

Add.

13. $17 + 9 =$ _____ $10 + 37 =$ _____ $22 + 28 =$ _____

14. $66 + 15 =$ _____ $45 + 15 =$ _____ $52 + 23 =$ _____

Subtract 2-Digit Numbers

THINK When there are not enough ones, regroup 1 ten as 10 ones.

Use Workmat 3 and ▭▭▭▭▭ ▫ . Subtract.

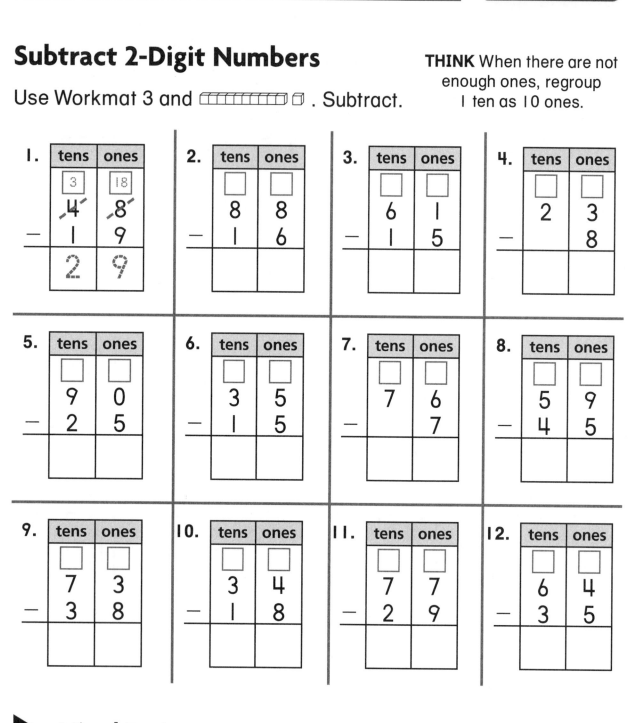

1.

tens	ones
3 ⁄4	18 ⁄8
− 1	9
2	9

2.

tens	ones
☐	☐
8	8
− 1	6

3.

tens	ones
☐	☐
6	1
− 1	5

4.

tens	ones
☐	☐
2	3
−	8

5.

tens	ones
☐	☐
9	0
− 2	5

6.

tens	ones
☐	☐
3	5
− 1	5

7.

tens	ones
☐	☐
7	6
−	7

8.

tens	ones
☐	☐
5	9
− 4	5

9.

tens	ones
☐	☐
7	3
− 3	8

10.

tens	ones
☐	☐
3	4
− 1	8

11.

tens	ones
☐	☐
7	7
− 2	9

12.

tens	ones
☐	☐
6	4
− 3	5

▶ **Mixed Review**

Count back to find the difference.

13. $94 - 10 = $ _____ $77 - 10 = $ _____ $73 - 20 = $ _____

14. $49 - 30 = $ _____ $62 - 20 = $ _____ $40 - 10 = $ _____

More 2-Digit Subtraction

Subtract. Regroup if you need to.

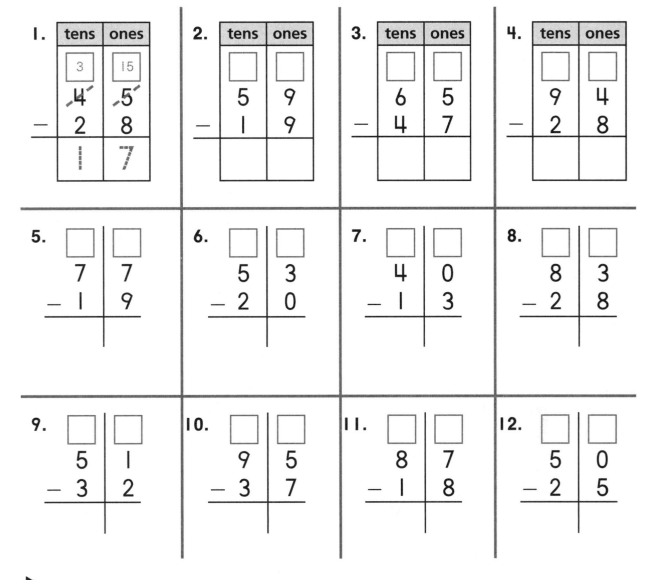

1.
tens	ones
3	15
4̸	5̸
− 2	8
1	7

2.
tens	ones
☐	☐
5	9
− 1	9

3.
tens	ones
☐	☐
6	5
− 4	7

4.
tens	ones
☐	☐
9	4
− 2	8

5.
```
   ☐  ☐
   7  7
 − 1  9
 _____
```

6.
```
   ☐  ☐
   5  3
 − 2  0
 _____
```

7.
```
   ☐  ☐
   4  0
 − 1  3
 _____
```

8.
```
   ☐  ☐
   8  3
 − 2  8
 _____
```

9.
```
   ☐  ☐
   5  1
 − 3  2
 _____
```

10.
```
   ☐  ☐
   9  5
 − 3  7
 _____
```

11.
```
   ☐  ☐
   8  7
 − 1  8
 _____
```

12.
```
   ☐  ☐
   5  0
 − 2  5
 _____
```

▶ **Mixed Review**

Write the missing numbers.

13. 14, ____, 18, 20, ____, ____, 26, ____

14. 9, ____, ____, 18, ____, 24, ____, 30

Rewrite 2-Digit Subtraction

Rewrite the numbers. Then subtract.

1. 61 − 37

```
   5  11
  -6  -1-
 - 3   7
 ─────────
   2   4
```

2. 77 − 71

3. 95 − 48

4. 40 − 29

5. 64 − 27

6. 62 − 22

7. 33 − 15

8. 62 − 33

9. 63 − 37

10. 86 − 8

11. 71 − 69

12. 82 − 34

▶ **Mixed Review**

Write the missing numbers.

13. 30, 40, ____, 60, ____, 80, 90

14. 14, ____, 34, ____, 54, ____, 74

Estimate Differences

Use the number line to round each number to the nearest ten. Estimate the difference.

THINK: If a number is halfway between two tens, round to the greater ten.

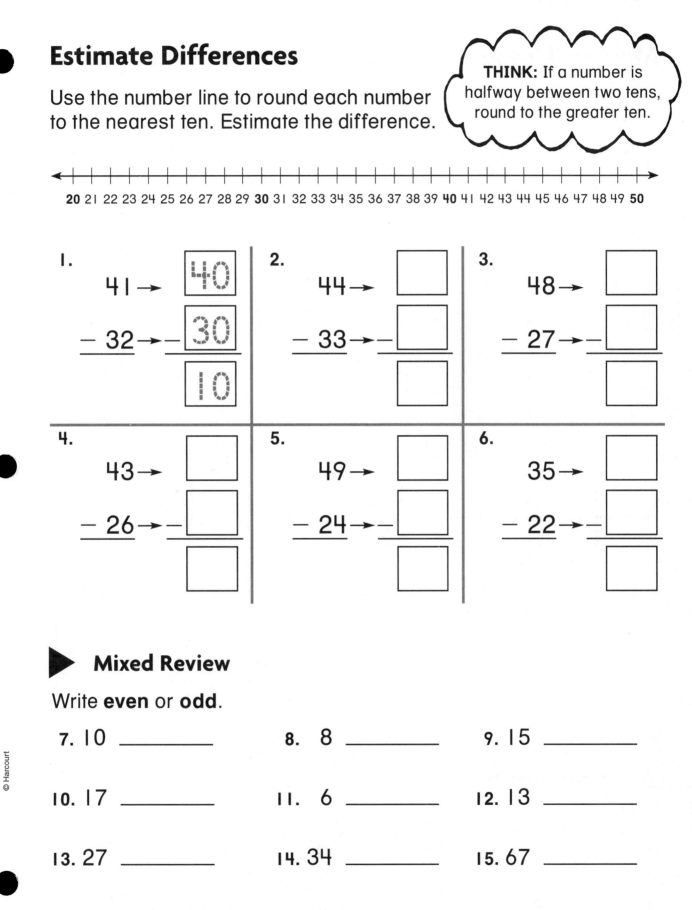

20 21 22 23 24 25 26 27 28 29 **30** 31 32 33 34 35 36 37 38 39 **40** 41 42 43 44 45 46 47 48 49 **50**

1.
$41 \rightarrow$ 40
$- 32 \rightarrow -$ 30
10

2.
$44 \rightarrow$ ☐
$- 33 \rightarrow -$ ☐
☐

3.
$48 \rightarrow$ ☐
$- 27 \rightarrow -$ ☐
☐

4.
$43 \rightarrow$ ☐
$- 26 \rightarrow -$ ☐
☐

5.
$49 \rightarrow$ ☐
$- 24 \rightarrow -$ ☐
☐

6.
$35 \rightarrow$ ☐
$- 22 \rightarrow -$ ☐
☐

▶ Mixed Review

Write **even** or **odd**.

7. 10 _____

8. 8 _____

9. 15 _____

10. 17 _____

11. 6 _____

12. 13 _____

13. 27 _____

14. 34 _____

15. 67 _____

Algebra: Use Addition to Check Subtraction

Subtract. Add to check.

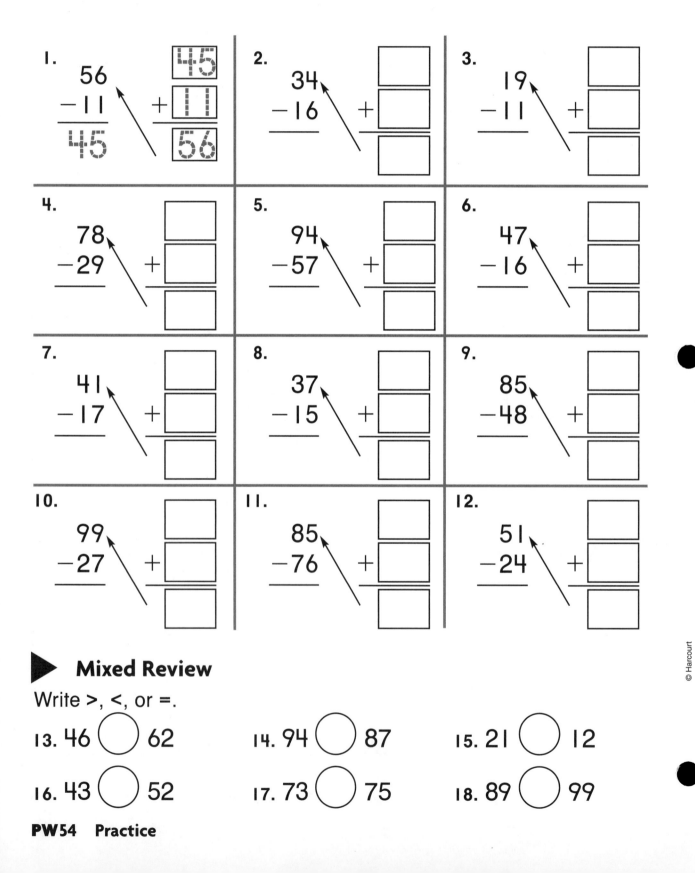

1.
$$\begin{array}{r} 56 \\ -11 \\ \hline 45 \end{array} \qquad + \begin{array}{r} 45 \\ 11 \\ \hline 56 \end{array}$$

2.
$$\begin{array}{r} 34 \\ -16 \\ \hline \end{array} \qquad + \begin{array}{r} \square \\ \square \\ \hline \square \end{array}$$

3.
$$\begin{array}{r} 19 \\ -11 \\ \hline \end{array} \qquad + \begin{array}{r} \square \\ \square \\ \hline \square \end{array}$$

4.
$$\begin{array}{r} 78 \\ -29 \\ \hline \end{array} \qquad + \begin{array}{r} \square \\ \square \\ \hline \square \end{array}$$

5.
$$\begin{array}{r} 94 \\ -57 \\ \hline \end{array} \qquad + \begin{array}{r} \square \\ \square \\ \hline \square \end{array}$$

6.
$$\begin{array}{r} 47 \\ -16 \\ \hline \end{array} \qquad + \begin{array}{r} \square \\ \square \\ \hline \square \end{array}$$

7.
$$\begin{array}{r} 41 \\ -17 \\ \hline \end{array} \qquad + \begin{array}{r} \square \\ \square \\ \hline \square \end{array}$$

8.
$$\begin{array}{r} 37 \\ -15 \\ \hline \end{array} \qquad + \begin{array}{r} \square \\ \square \\ \hline \square \end{array}$$

9.
$$\begin{array}{r} 85 \\ -48 \\ \hline \end{array} \qquad + \begin{array}{r} \square \\ \square \\ \hline \square \end{array}$$

10.
$$\begin{array}{r} 99 \\ -27 \\ \hline \end{array} \qquad + \begin{array}{r} \square \\ \square \\ \hline \square \end{array}$$

11.
$$\begin{array}{r} 85 \\ -76 \\ \hline \end{array} \qquad + \begin{array}{r} \square \\ \square \\ \hline \square \end{array}$$

12.
$$\begin{array}{r} 51 \\ -24 \\ \hline \end{array} \qquad + \begin{array}{r} \square \\ \square \\ \hline \square \end{array}$$

▶ **Mixed Review**

Write >, <, or =.

13. 46 ◯ 62

14. 94 ◯ 87

15. 21 ◯ 12

16. 43 ◯ 52

17. 73 ◯ 75

18. 89 ◯ 99

Problem Solving: Choose the Computational Method

Choose a method and solve the problem.

Use paper and pencil.	Use a calculator.	Count back.	Use base ten blocks.

1. Anna collects sports stamps. She has 67 stamps. She gives 14 away. How many stamps does Anna have left?

   _____ stamps

2. A page in a stamp book holds 32 stamps. Mark has 20 stamps. How many more stamps does he need to fill the page?

   _____ stamps

3. Alma received 21 stamps on her birthday. Her grandmother gave her 12 of them. How many stamps were not from her grandmother?

   _____ stamps

4. Alfredo has 83 stamps in his collection. He sends 29 stamps to his cousin. How many stamps does Alfredo have left?

   _____ stamps

© Harcourt

Different Ways to Add

Choose the best way to add. Find the sum.

1. $\begin{array}{r} 57 \\ + 30 \\ \hline 87 \end{array}$

2. $\begin{array}{r} 14 \\ + 13 \\ \hline \end{array}$

3. $\begin{array}{r} 62 \\ + 4 \\ \hline \end{array}$

4. $\begin{array}{r} 44 \\ + 36 \\ \hline \end{array}$

5. $\begin{array}{r} 29 \\ + 8 \\ \hline \end{array}$

6. $\begin{array}{r} 21 \\ + 40 \\ \hline \end{array}$

7. $\begin{array}{r} 18 \\ + 18 \\ \hline \end{array}$

8. $\begin{array}{r} 24 \\ + 5 \\ \hline \end{array}$

9. $\begin{array}{r} 65 \\ + 10 \\ \hline \end{array}$

10. $\begin{array}{r} 12 \\ + 48 \\ \hline \end{array}$

11. $\begin{array}{r} 81 \\ + 10 \\ \hline \end{array}$

12. $\begin{array}{r} 26 \\ + 50 \\ \hline \end{array}$

13. $\begin{array}{r} 38 \\ + 13 \\ \hline \end{array}$

14. $\begin{array}{r} 52 \\ + 11 \\ \hline \end{array}$

15. $\begin{array}{r} 37 \\ + 36 \\ \hline \end{array}$

16. $\begin{array}{r} 14 \\ + 67 \\ \hline \end{array}$

17. $\begin{array}{r} 6 \\ + 40 \\ \hline \end{array}$

18. $\begin{array}{r} 18 \\ + 3 \\ \hline \end{array}$

19. $\begin{array}{r} 48 \\ + 27 \\ \hline \end{array}$

20. $\begin{array}{r} 49 \\ + 30 \\ \hline \end{array}$

▶ **Mixed Review**

Count back to subtract.

21. $48 - 10 = $ _____   22. $70 - 10 = $ _____   23. $91 - 10 = $ _____

24. $37 - 10 = $ _____   25. $89 - 10 = $ _____   26. $16 - 10 = $ _____

© Harcourt

Practice 2-Digit Addition

Toss a number cube with the numbers 1, 2, and 3
to fill in the boxes. Then add.

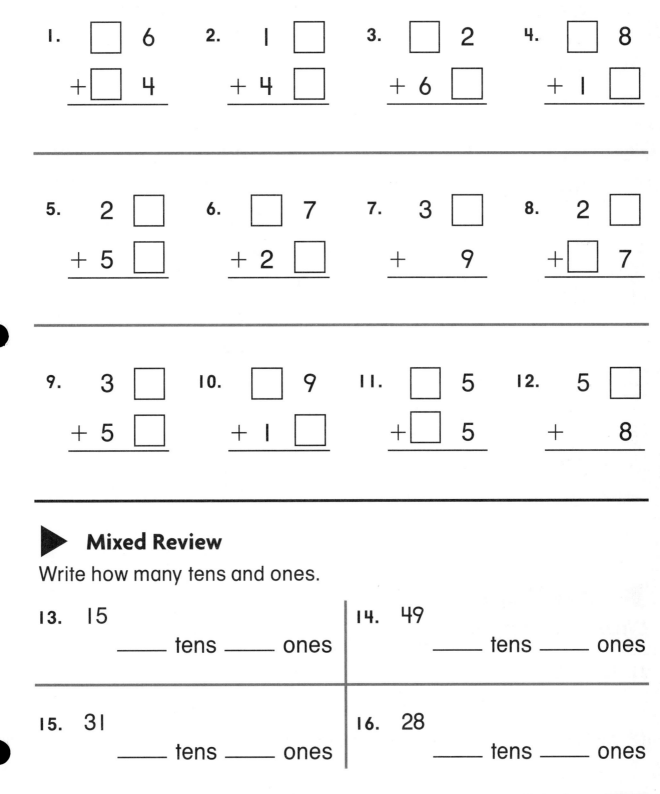

1. ☐ 6
  + ☐ 4

2. 1 ☐
  + 4 ☐

3. ☐ 2
  + 6 ☐

4. ☐ 8
  + 1 ☐

5. 2 ☐
  + 5 ☐

6. ☐ 7
  + 2 ☐

7. 3 ☐
  +   9

8. 2 ☐
  + ☐ 7

9. 3 ☐
  + 5 ☐

10. ☐ 9
  + 1 ☐

11. ☐ 5
  + ☐ 5

12. 5 ☐
  +   8

▶ **Mixed Review**

Write how many tens and ones.

13. 15
  ____ tens ____ ones

14. 49
  ____ tens ____ ones

15. 31
  ____ tens ____ ones

16. 28
  ____ tens ____ ones

Column Addition

Add.

1. 34 ⟩10
    16 ⟩15
    + 25
    75

2. 18
    31
    + 41

3.   7
    57
    + 11

4. 26
    26
    + 2

5. 15
    19
    + 33

6. 41
     9
    + 17

7. 55
    15
    + 8

8. 29
    12
    + 24

9. 33
    16
    + 49

10. 18
    30
    + 5

11. 21
    56
    + 12

12.   6
    16
    + 26

13. 72
    16
    + 11

14. 16
    29
    + 31

15. 41
     4
    + 35

16. 17
     3
    + 28

▶ **Mixed Review**

Write the missing addend.

17. $8 +$ _____ $= 15$ $15 - 8 =$ _____

18. _____ $+ 6 = 12$ $12 - 6 =$ _____

Different Ways to Subtract

Subtract using different ways.
Then use the code to read the message.

I – A	2 – B	3 – C	4 – D	5 – E
6 – F	7 – G	8 – H	9 – I	10 – J
11 – K	12 – L	13 – M	14 – N	15 – O
16 – P	17 – Q	18 – R	19 – S	20 – T
21 – U	22 – V	23 – W	24 – X	25 – Y
26 – Z				

What's gray and has a trunk?

$$\begin{array}{cccccc} \overset{2\;10}{\cancel{30}} & 26 & 18 & 50 & 44 & 68 \\ -29 & -13 & -\;3 & -29 & -25 & -63 \end{array}$$

   I

   A

$$\begin{array}{ccccccc} 19 & 42 & 50 & 72 & 36 & 40 & 24 \\ -\;4 & -28 & -49 & -52 & -18 & -31 & -\;8 \end{array}$$

_____ _____ _____ _____ _____ _____ _____

_____ _____ _____ _____ _____ _____ _____

▶ **Mixed Review**

Add.

14. $71 + 19 =$ _____ $27 + 27 =$ _____ $14 + 23 =$ _____

15. $25 + 26 =$ _____ $7 + 18 =$ _____ $37 + 30 =$ _____

Practice 2-Digit Subtraction

Circle the exercises in which you will need to regroup.
Then subtract.

1.   67
   − 32
   ─────
    35

2.   34
   − 13
   ─────

3.   62
   − 48
   ─────

4.   44
   − 16
   ─────

5.   76
   − 40
   ─────

6.   61
   − 28
   ─────

7.   79
   − 18
   ─────

8.   43
   − 29
   ─────

9.   65
   − 38
   ─────

10.   95
    − 42
   ─────

11.   81
    − 50
   ─────

12.   56
    − 15
   ─────

13.   74
    − 36
   ─────

14.   82
    − 55
   ─────

15.   60
    − 26
   ─────

16.   54
    − 26
   ─────

17.   86
    − 43
   ─────

18.   92
    − 65
   ─────

19.   40
    − 27
   ─────

20.   67
    − 19
   ─────

 Mixed Review

Draw a line through any information you do not
need. Then solve.

21. Zoe has 14 pennies, 19 dimes, and 3 dollar bills to
    spend at the store. How many coins does Zoe have?

_____ coins

Mixed Practice

Circle the **+** or **−**. Then solve.

1. 95 ⊝ 32 **63**	2. 52 + 27	3. 67 − 8	4. 78 − 59	5. 86 − 18
6. 75 + 24	7. 25 + 36	8. 94 − 48	9. 46 + 24	10. 50 + 38
11. 74 − 12	12. 52 − 49	13. 89 − 15	14. 44 + 37	15. 62 − 55
16. 22 + 77	17. 27 + 25	18. 42 + 37	19. 60 − 41	20. 56 − 18

▶ **Mixed Review**

Find the sum or difference.

21. $8 + 7 =$ _____   22. $7 + 8 =$ _____   23. $15 - 8 =$ _____

24. $15 - 7 =$ _____   25. $7 + 6 =$ _____   26. $6 + 7 =$ _____

27. $13 - 6 =$ _____   28. $13 - 7 =$ _____   29. $9 + 7 =$ _____

30. $7 + 9 =$ _____   31. $16 - 7 =$ _____   32. $16 - 9 =$ _____

© Harcourt

Problem Solving • Work Backward

Work backward to solve each problem.

1. Robbie gave her friend 38 seashells. She has 12 left. How many seashells did she start with?

   Start with 12, and add back 38.

   __50__ seashells

2. Dina and Olly picked 24 flowers from the garden. Now there are 47 flowers left in the garden. How many flowers were in the garden to start with?

   _____ flowers

3. Wesley made some frogs out of paper. He gave his brother 10 paper frogs. He gave his sister 15 paper frogs. He has 29 frogs left. How many frogs did Wesley make?

   _____ frogs

4. Some children were on the soccer field. 12 children went into the gym. 6 more children sat on the bench. Now there are 17 children on the field. How many children were on the field to start with?

   _____ children

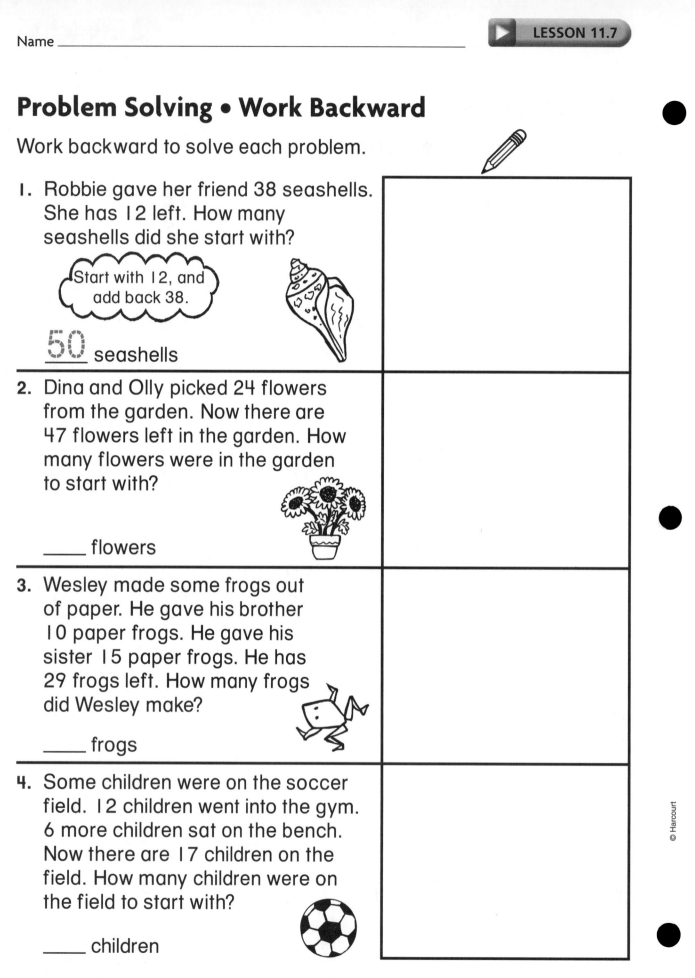

● # Pennies, Nickels, and Dimes

Count on to find the total amount.

1.

___10___ ¢, ___ ¢, ___ ¢, ___ ¢, ___ ¢, ___ ¢   [28] ¢

2.

___ ¢, ___ ¢, ___ ¢, ___ ¢, ___ ¢, ___ ¢   [ ] ¢

● **3.**

___ ¢, ___ ¢, ___ ¢, ___ ¢, ___ ¢, ___ ¢   [ ] ¢

4.

___ ¢, ___ ¢, ___ ¢, ___ ¢, ___ ¢, ___ ¢   [ ] ¢

▶ **Mixed Review**

Complete.

5. 12, ___, 18, 21   25, 30, ___, 40

● 6. ___, 50, 60, 70   32, ___, 36, 38

Quarters and Half Dollars

Count on to find the total amount.

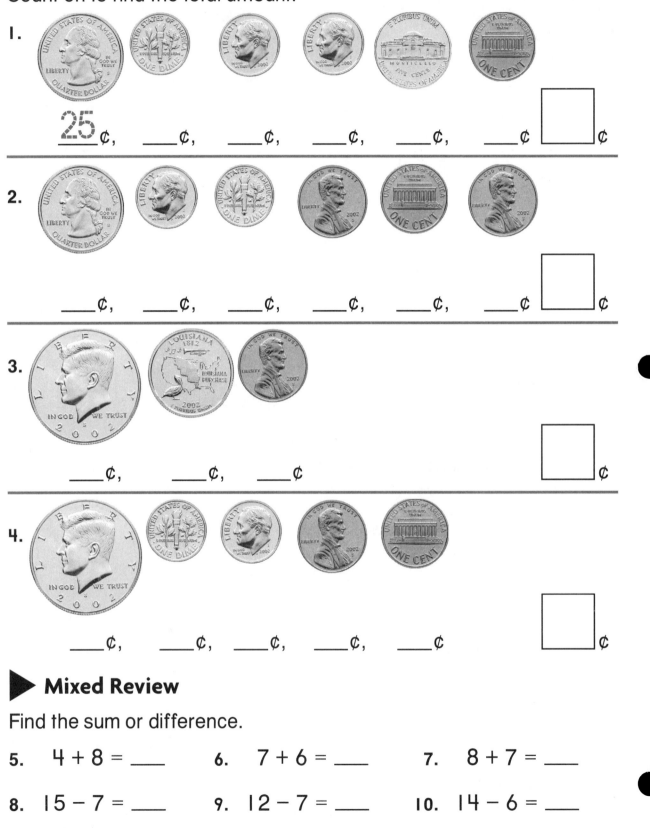

1.   25¢,   ____¢,   ____¢,   ____¢,   ____¢,   ____¢   ☐¢

2.   ____¢,   ____¢,   ____¢,   ____¢,   ____¢,   ____¢   ☐¢

3.   ____¢,   ____¢,   ____¢   ☐¢

4.   ____¢,   ____¢,   ____¢,   ____¢,   ____¢   ☐¢

▶ Mixed Review

Find the sum or difference.

5. 4 + 8 = ____   **6.** 7 + 6 = ____   **7.** 8 + 7 = ____

8. 15 − 7 = ____   **9.** 12 − 7 = ____   **10.** 14 − 6 = ____

© Harcourt

Count Collections

Draw and label the coins in order from
greatest to least value. Write the total amount.

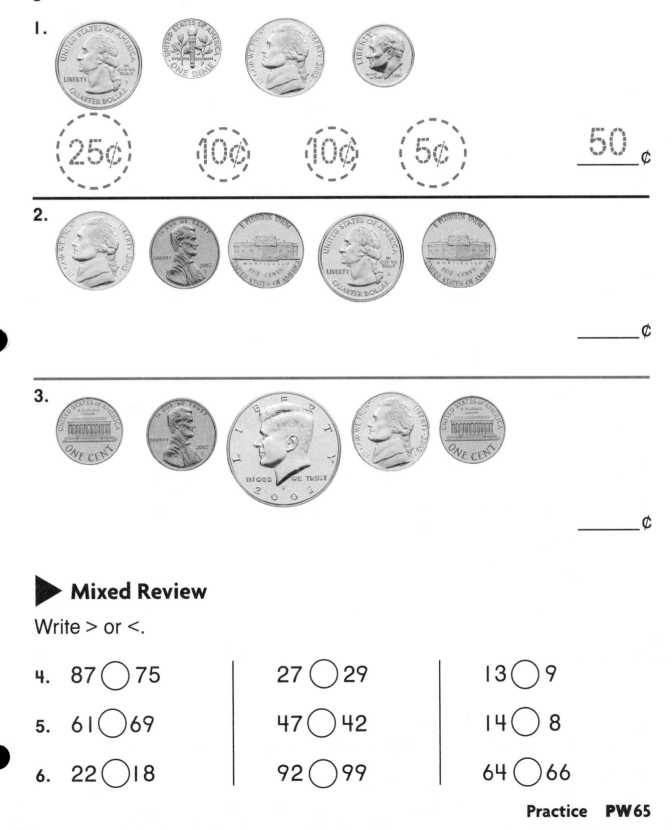

1.

25¢   10¢   10¢   5¢   50 ¢

2.

_____ ¢

3.

_____ ¢

▶ Mixed Review

Write > or <.

4. 87 ◯ 75   27 ◯ 29   13 ◯ 9

5. 61 ◯ 69   47 ◯ 42   14 ◯ 8

6. 22 ◯ 18   92 ◯ 99   64 ◯ 66

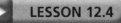

1 Dollar

Use coins. Show other ways to make $1.00.
Write how many of each coin.

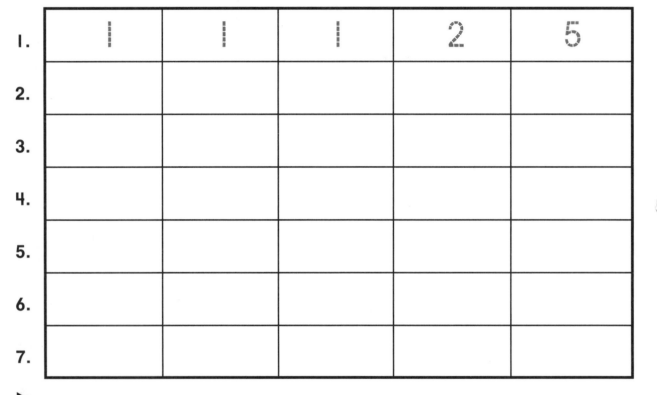

1.	1	1	1	2	5
2.					
3.					
4.					
5.					
6.					
7.					

▶ **Mixed Review**

Write **even** or **odd**.

8. 17 _____   18 _____   19 _____

9. 26 _____   38 _____   30 _____

Add Money

Rewrite the numbers in each problem.
Then add.

Remember:
Write the ¢.

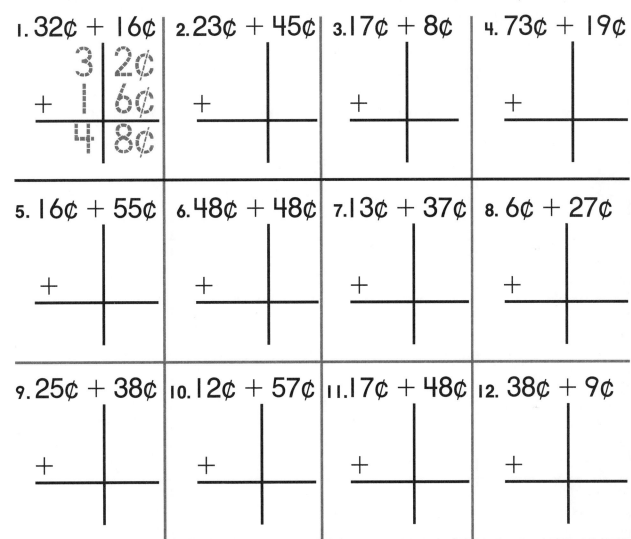

1. 32¢ + 16¢

$$
\begin{array}{r}
3\,|\,2¢ \\
+\ 1\,|\,6¢ \\
\hline
4\,|\,8¢
\end{array}
$$

2. 23¢ + 45¢

3. 17¢ + 8¢

4. 73¢ + 19¢

5. 16¢ + 55¢

6. 48¢ + 48¢

7. 13¢ + 37¢

8. 6¢ + 27¢

9. 25¢ + 38¢

10. 12¢ + 57¢

11. 17¢ + 48¢

12. 38¢ + 9¢

▶ **Mixed Review**

Subtract.

13. 27 − 14 = ____   75 − 10 = ____

14. 19 − 11 = ____   43 − 15 = ____

15. 36 − 18 = ____   51 − 36 = ____

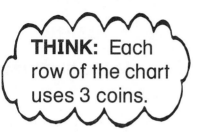

Problem Solving • Make a List

Tim has 3 coins in his pouch. None of the coins is worth more than 25¢. None of the coins is a penny. How much money could he have? Make a list to find out.

THINK: Each row of the chart uses 3 coins.

quarters	dimes	nickels	total amount
3	0	0	75¢
2	1	0	
2	0	1	

© Harcourt

Make the Same Amounts

Use coins. Show the amount of money in two ways.
Draw and label each coin.

1. 65¢	10¢ 10¢ 25¢ 10¢ 10¢	
2. 47¢		
3. 89¢		

▶ **Mixed Review**

Solve.

4. 12 − 3 = ____   9 + 5 = ____   7 + 7 = ____

5. 12 − 9 = ____   16 − 8 = ____   13 − 13 = ____

6. 7 + 9 = ____   9 + 9 = ____   9 + 8 = ____

Algebra: Same Amounts Using the Fewest Coins

Write the amount. Then show the same amount with the
fewest coins. Draw and label each coin.

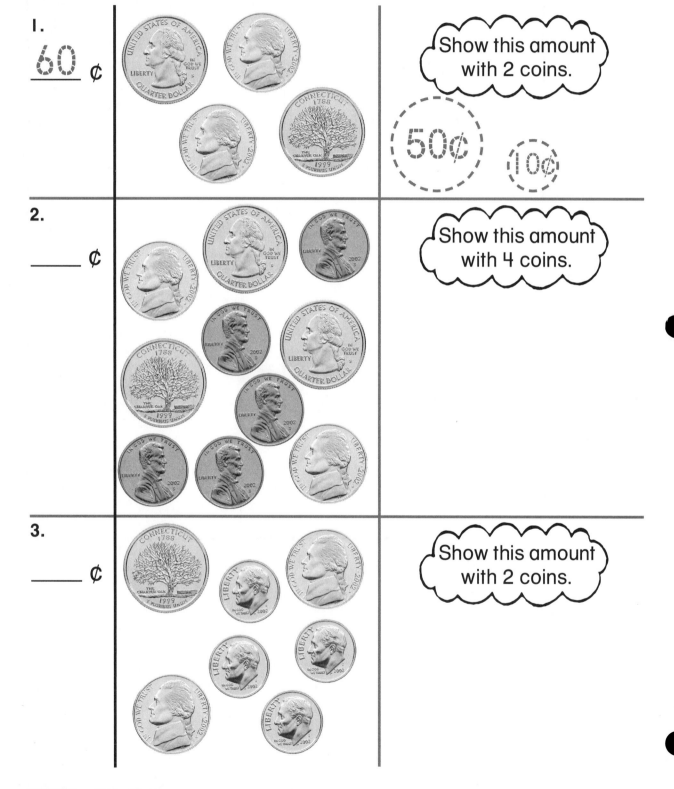

1.

___60___ ¢

Show this amount
with 2 coins.

50¢   10¢

2.

_____ ¢

Show this amount
with 4 coins.

3.

_____ ¢

Show this amount
with 2 coins.

Compare Amounts

Write the amounts of money. Then write >, <, or =.

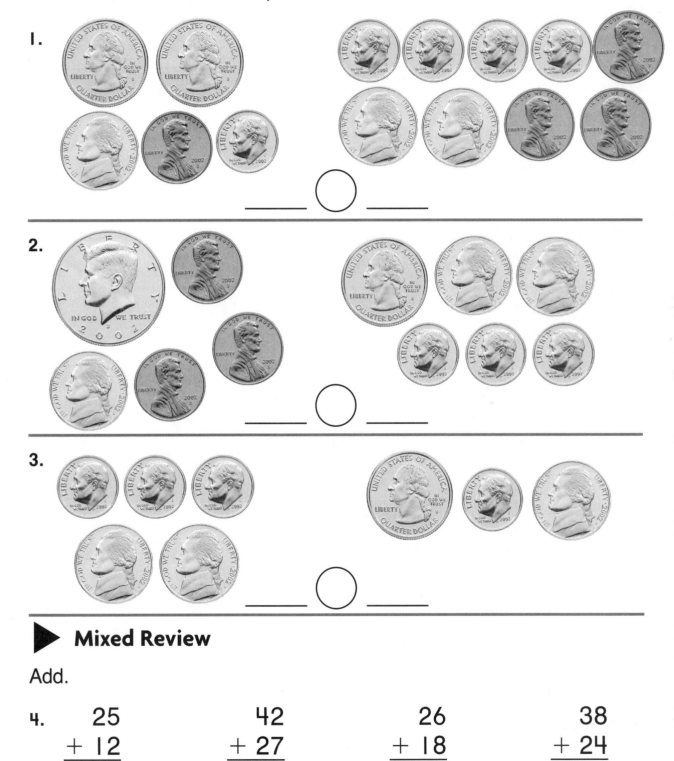

1.

_____ ◯ _____

2.

_____ ◯ _____

3.

_____ ◯ _____

▶ **Mixed Review**

Add.

4.
$\begin{array}{r} 25 \\ + 12 \\ \hline \end{array}$ $\begin{array}{r} 42 \\ + 27 \\ \hline \end{array}$ $\begin{array}{r} 26 \\ + 18 \\ \hline \end{array}$ $\begin{array}{r} 38 \\ + 24 \\ \hline \end{array}$

Name _____

Compare Amounts to Prices

Write the amount.
Write the names and
prices of two foods
you could buy.

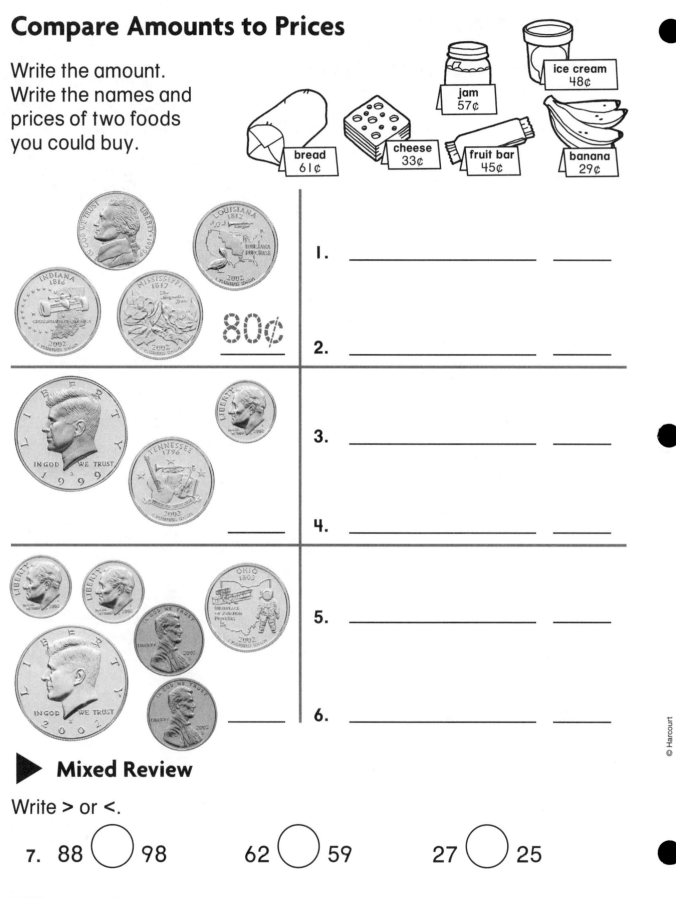

jam 57¢

ice cream 48¢

bread 61¢

cheese 33¢

fruit bar 45¢

banana 29¢

80¢

1. _____ _____

2. _____ _____

3. _____ _____

4. _____ _____

5. _____ _____

6. _____ _____

▶ **Mixed Review**

Write > or <.

7. 88 ◯ 98   62 ◯ 59   27 ◯ 25

Name _____

Make Change to $1.00

Count on from the price to find the change.

1. You have 55¢. You buy

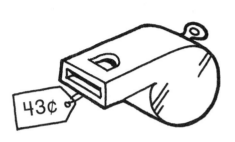

43¢

__44__ ¢, __45__ ¢, __55__ ¢

Your change is __12¢__.

---

2. You have 50¢. You buy

43¢

__44__ ¢, _____ ¢, _____ ¢

Your change is _____.

---

3. You have 70¢. You buy

57¢

__58__ ¢, _____ ¢, _____ ¢, _____ ¢

Your change is _____.

▶ **Mixed Review**

Solve.

4.   7 + ____ = 15   6 + ____ = 14   6 + ____ = 12

5.   16 − ____ = 8   12 − ____ = 7   14 − ____ = 8

6.   9 + ____ = 15   5 + ____ = 14   9 + ____ = 18

Subtract Money

Rewrite the numbers.
Then subtract.

REMEMBER:
Write the ¢.

1. 87¢ − 34¢

	8	7¢
−	3	4¢
	5	3¢

2. 74¢ − 54¢

3. 62¢ − 15¢

4. 53¢ − 39¢

5. 77¢ − 9¢

6. 41¢ − 28¢

7. 79¢ − 6¢

8. 22¢ − 19¢

9. 42¢ − 37¢

10. 21¢ − 17¢

11. 55¢ − 40¢

12. 48¢ − 16¢

▶ **Mixed Review**

Add or subtract.

13. 54
   + 9

14. 57
   − 35

15. 23
   − 7

16. 32
   + 14

17. 45
   − 16

18. 72
   + 12

19. 39
   + 19

20. 92
   − 30

© Harcourt

Problem Solving • Use Estimation

Estimate the cost of two items. Check
to see if your estimate is reasonable.
Draw the two items you buy.

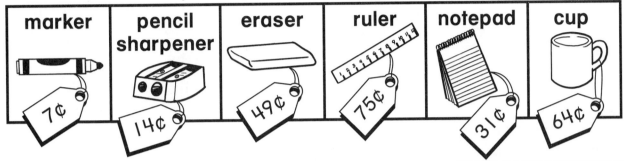

marker	pencil sharpener	eraser	ruler	notepad	cup
7¢	14¢	49¢	75¢	31¢	64¢

1. You want to spend no more than 60¢.

Estimate	Check
50¢ +10¢ 60¢	

2. You want to spend no more than 30¢.

Estimate	Check

3. You want to spend no more than 50¢.

Estimate	Check

© Harcourt

Explore 1 Minute

About how long will it take?

Circle the better estimate.

1. to kick a ball — more than
1 minute / **(less than
1 minute)**

2. to read a book — more than
1 minute / less than
1 minute

3. to cut the grass — more than
1 minute / less than
1 minute

4. to touch your toes — more than
1 minute / less than
1 minute

5. to cook soup — more than
1 minute / less than
1 minute

6. to write your name — more than
1 minute / less than
1 minute

▶ **Mixed Review**

Add.

7. $26 + 26 =$ _____ $15 + 7 =$ _____ $8 + 31 =$ _____

8. $39 + 41 =$ _____ $20 + 16 =$ _____ $28 + 14 =$ _____

9. $17 + 7 =$ _____ $75 + 24 =$ _____ $8 + 88 =$ _____

Time to the Hour

Draw the minute hand and the hour hand.
Write the time another way.

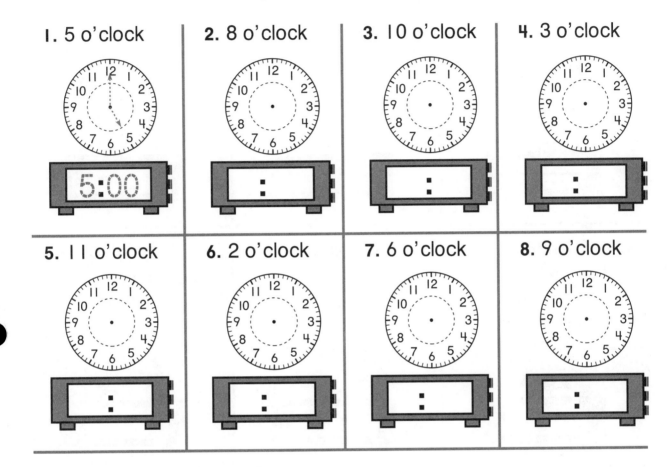

1. 5 o'clock **2.** 8 o'clock **3.** 10 o'clock **4.** 3 o'clock

5:00

5. 11 o'clock **6.** 2 o'clock **7.** 6 o'clock **8.** 9 o'clock

▶ **Mixed Review**

Write the value.

9.

____ ¢

10.

____ ¢

Time to the Half-Hour

Draw the minute hand.
Write the time another way.

1. 30 minutes after 5

5:30

2. eight-thirty

3. half past 6

4. 30 minutes before 2

5. four-thirty

6. 30 minutes after 10

▶ **Mixed Review**

Solve.

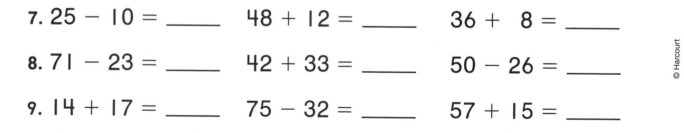

7. $25 - 10 =$ _____ $48 + 12 =$ _____ $36 + 8 =$ _____

8. $71 - 23 =$ _____ $42 + 33 =$ _____ $50 - 26 =$ _____

9. $14 + 17 =$ _____ $75 - 32 =$ _____ $57 + 15 =$ _____

Time to 15 Minutes

Draw the minute hand to show the time.
Write the time another way.

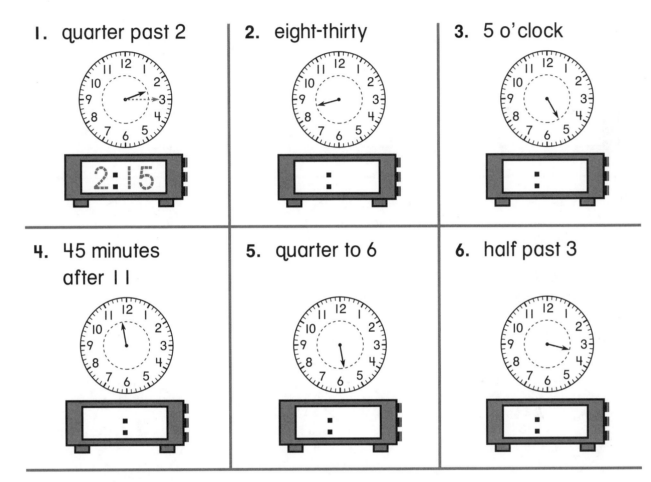

1. quarter past 2

2. eight-thirty

3. 5 o'clock

4. 45 minutes after 11

5. quarter to 6

6. half past 3

▶ **Mixed Review**

You have 75¢. Tell how much change you will get.

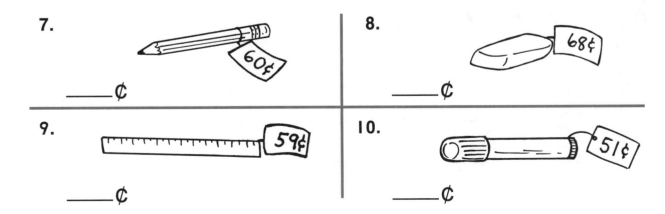

7. _____ ¢

8. _____ ¢

9. _____ ¢

10. _____ ¢

© Harcourt

Minutes

Write the time another way.

1.

1:23

2.

:

3.

:

4.

:

5.

:

6.

:

7.

:

8.

:

9.

:

▶ **Mixed Review**

Add.

10.

15	23	72	9	10
22	41	10	25	36
+ 31	+ 17	+ 8	+ 38	+ 17

© Harcourt

Problem Solving • Use a Model

Use a 🕐 to help solve the problem.
Write how much time has passed.

1. Sam begins to play tennis at 3:30. He finishes playing at 4:30. How much time has passed?

_____ hour

2. June begins to eat lunch at 12:10. She finishes at 12:30. How much time has passed?

_____ minutes

3. Bill takes a nap at 3:15. He wakes up at 4:00. How much time has passed?

_____ minutes

4. Sue and her family take a trip to the beach. They leave home at 9:15. They get to the beach at 12:15. How much time has passed?

_____ hours

5. Allison begins to read her book at 4:00. She finishes the book at 6:00. How much time has passed?

_____ hours

6. Ali delivers newspapers. He begins at 6:30. He finishes at 7:30. How much time has passed?

_____ hours

7. Andy takes a bath at 7:45. He gets out of the bath at 8:00. How much time has passed?

_____ minutes

8. The children play in the yard. They begin to play at 11:30. They finish at 2:30. How much time has passed?

_____ hours

Sequencing Months

Use the calendar to answer the questions.

1. Which month is the last month of the year?   December

2. Which is the third month of the year?   _____

3. Which month is just after July?   _____

4. Which month is just before February?   _____

5. Which is the eleventh month?   _____

6. Which month is just before the tenth month?   _____

▶ **Mixed Review**

Solve.

7. $64 - 7 =$ _____ $57 - 9 =$ _____ $28 - 9 =$ _____

8. $39 - 9 =$ _____ $42 - 3 =$ _____ $18 - 7 =$ _____

Dates on a Calendar

Use the calendar to answer the questions.

1. What is the date of the first Monday?

July 7

2. What is the date of the fifth Tuesday?

_____

3. What is the day and date one week after July 16?

JULY						
Sunday	Monday	Tuesday	Wednesday	Thursday	Friday	Saturday
		1	2	3	4 Independence Day	5
6	7	8	9	10	11	12
13	14	15	16	17	18	19
20	21	22	23	24	25	26
27	28	29	30	31		

_____ , _____

4. What is the day and date three weeks before July 26?

_____ , _____

5. On which day will the next month start?

_____

6. What is the date two weeks after Independence Day?

_____

▶ **Mixed Review**

Solve.

7.

35¢	91¢	74¢	28¢
− 22¢	− 67¢	− 25¢	− 19¢

Days, Weeks, Months, Years

Write **more than**, **less than**, or **the same as** to complete the sentence.

Time Relationships
There are 7 days in 1 week.
There are 28, 29, 30, or 31 days in 1 month.
There are about 4 weeks in 1 month.
There are 52 weeks in 1 year.
There are 12 months in 1 year.

1. Steve plays ball after school every day for 4 days in a row.

    This is ___less than___ 1 week.

2. Pam walks her dog every day for 1 month.

    This is _____ 35 days.

3. Tim goes to summer camp for 45 days.

    This is _____ 1 month.

4. Maya's family goes on vacation for 7 days.

    This is _____ 1 week.

5. The soccer season lasts 2 months.

    This is _____ 7 weeks.

▶ **Mixed Review**

Write the time another way.

6.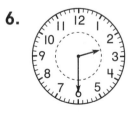

© Harcourt

Estimate Time

About how long will it take?
Circle the amount of time that makes sense.

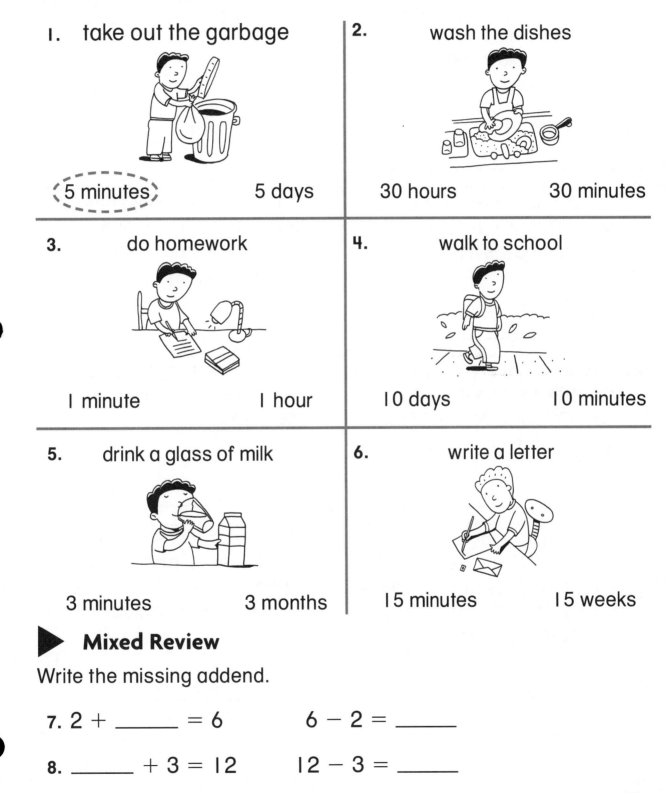

1. take out the garbage

(5 minutes)   5 days

2. wash the dishes

30 hours   30 minutes

3. do homework

1 minute   1 hour

4. walk to school

10 days   10 minutes

5. drink a glass of milk

3 minutes   3 months

6. write a letter

15 minutes   15 weeks

▶ **Mixed Review**

Write the missing addend.

7. $2 +$ _____ $= 6$ $6 - 2 =$ _____

8. _____ $+ 3 = 12$ $12 - 3 =$ _____

Problem Solving • Use a Table

Use the calendar to solve the problems.

1. Winter vacation ended 4 days ago. Today is January 9. On what date did winter vacation end?

   January 5

JANUARY						
Sunday	Monday	Tuesday	Wednesday	Thursday	Friday	Saturday
	1	2	3	4	5	6
7	8	9	10	11	12	13
14	15	16	17	18	19	20
21	22	23	24	25	26	27
28	29	30	31			

2. Lucas has a math test in 5 days. Today is January 21. On what day is his test?

   _____

3. Linda has dance lessons on January 6, 13, 20, and 27. On what day does she have dance lessons?

   _____

4. Today is January 15. Alice saw her grandmother 2 weeks ago. On what date did Alice see her grandmother?

   _____

5. Lisa's basketball game is on February 1. On what day is the game?

   _____

6. David's violin recital is January 27. He has practice on the Wednesday before the recital. On what date is the practice?

   _____

7. Mike's birthday is 12 days after Mara's birthday. Mara's birthday is January 11. On what date is Mike's birthday?

   _____

Problem Solving • Make a Graph

Alicia asked her classmates which of five evening activities they liked best. She made a tally table to keep track of their answers.

Evening Activities We Like	
Activity	**Tally**
read a book	HHT II
watch TV	HHT III
play with toys	IIII
use the computer	HHT HHT
play sports	HHT I

1. Use Alicia's tally table to make a bar graph.

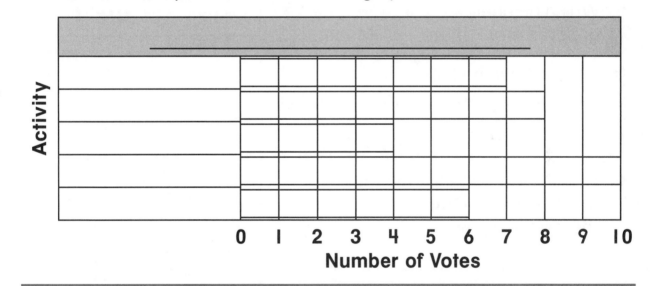

2. Use the bar graph to order the activities from the one that received the most votes to the one that received the fewest votes.

Most _____

_____

_____

_____

_____

Range, Median, and Mode

Use 🎲 to show the tallies.
Write the numbers in order from least to greatest.

1. _5_ , _5_ , _6_ , _8_ , _10_

Number of Books Read	
Name	**Tally**
Tina	ЖHT III
Gary	ЖHT
Lupe	ЖHT
Tisha	ЖHT ЖHT
Julio	ЖHT I

2. Find the difference between the greatest number and the least number.

   ____ – ____ = ____   Range ____

3. Which number is in the middle?   Median ____

4. Which number appears most often?   Mode ____

Use 🎲 to show the tallies.
Write the numbers in order from least to greatest.

5. _____ , _____ , _____ , _____ , _____

Books We Enjoy	
Type of Book	**Tally**
Mystery	ЖHT
Fairy Tale	ЖHT I
Fiction	ЖHT II
Biography	ЖHT
Nonfiction	III

6. Find the difference between the greatest number and the least number.

   ____ – ____ = ____   Range ____

7. Which number is in the middle?   Median ____

8. Which number appears most?   Mode ____

▶ **Mixed Review**

Write the sum.

9. $8 + 4 + 2 =$ ____

10. $7 + 7 + 5 =$ ____

Algebra: Locate Points on a Grid

Mark each point on the grid.

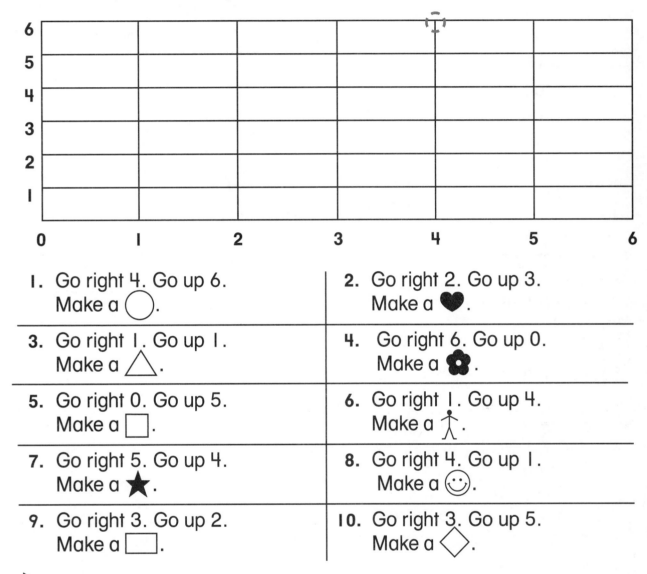

1. Go right 4. Go up 6.
   Make a ◯.

2. Go right 2. Go up 3.
   Make a ❤.

3. Go right 1. Go up 1.
   Make a △.

4. Go right 6. Go up 0.
   Make a ✿.

5. Go right 0. Go up 5.
   Make a ☐.

6. Go right 1. Go up 4.
   Make a 🏃.

7. Go right 5. Go up 4.
   Make a ★.

8. Go right 4. Go up 1.
   Make a ☺.

9. Go right 3. Go up 2.
   Make a ▭.

10. Go right 3. Go up 5.
    Make a ◇.

▶ **Mixed Review**

Write the time.

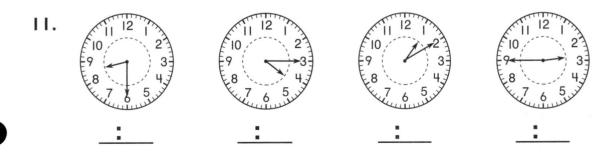

11.

___ : ___   ___ : ___   ___ : ___   ___ : ___

Read Line Graphs

Use the line graph to answer the questions.

1. How many ducks were at the pond on Thursday? __20__

2. How many ducks were at the pond on Friday? _____

3. How many more ducks were at the pond on Wednesday than on Monday? _____

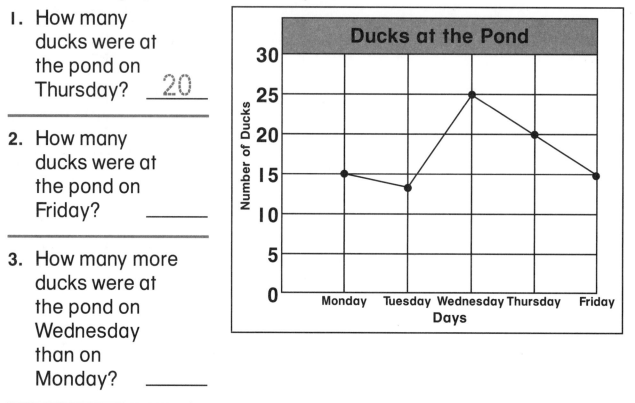

4. How many fewer ducks were at the pond on Friday than on Wednesday? _____

5. On which day were there the most ducks? _____

6. On which day were there the fewest ducks? _____

▶ Mixed Review

Subtract. Regroup if you need to.

7.	8.	9.	10.	11.
35¢	42¢	82¢	45¢	92¢
− 24¢	− 7¢	− 67¢	− 42¢	− 18¢

Problem Solving • Make a Prediction

Make a prediction.

1. Sherona grabbed a handful of crayons from a box. What prediction can she make about which color crayon there is the fewest of in the box?

   Prediction: The fewest crayons are yellow.

Crayons in the Box	
Color	**Tally**
blue	ЖHT II
red	ЖHT
green	ЖHT I
yellow	II
black	ЖHT ЖHT II

2. Jimmy pulled some stickers from a bag. What prediction can he make about which kind of sticker there is the fewest of in the bag?

   Prediction: _____

   _____

   _____

Stickers in the Bag	
Sticker	**Tally**
animal	I
star	IIII
rainbow	ЖHT
happy face	ЖHT II

3. Jessie pulled some toys from the box. What prediction can she make about which toy there is the most of in the box?

   Prediction: _____

   _____

   _____

Toys in the Box	
Toy	**Tally**
animal	ЖHT
car	ЖHT III
doll	III
truck	I

© Harcourt

Interpreting Outcomes of Games

These are the results of 15 spins
of this spinner.

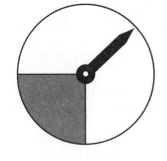

spin	1	2	3	4	5	6	7	8	9	10	11	12	13	14	15
outcome	w	w	g	w	w	w	g	w	g	w	w	w	g	w	w

Use the chart to complete the tally
table. Then answer the questions.

Outcomes of the Spins	
Color	Tally
white	
gray	

1. What are the possible outcomes for this spinner? _white, gray_

_____

2. How many times was gray the outcome? _____

_____

3. Which color was the outcome more often? _____

_____

4. If you used the spinner again, which outcome
   would you predict? _____

▶ **Mixed Review**

Write the time.

5.

_____

6.

_____

7.
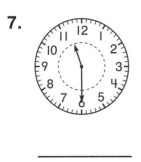

_____

Name _____

Certain or Impossible

If ◯ is a certain outcome, write **Yes**.
If ◯ is an impossible outcome, write **No**.

		Certain	Impossible
1.	A ▽ ▽ □ □□□□	no	
2.	B ▽ ○ ○○○		
3.	C ▽▽▽ ▽▽▽		
4.	D ○○ ○○○		

5. Use **yellow** ▷. Color the bag from which pulling a triangle is certain.

---

6. Use **blue** ▷. Color the bag from which pulling a triangle is impossible.

▶ Mixed Review

Mark each point on the grid.

7. Go right 3. Go up 2. Make a C.

8. Go right 1. Go up 5. Make an A.

9. Go right 2. Go up 3. Make a B.

10. Go right 5. Go up 1. Make a D.

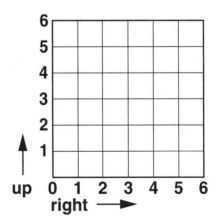

Likely or Unlikely

Write **likely** or **unlikely** to tell the chances of pulling
a ○ and a △ from each bag.

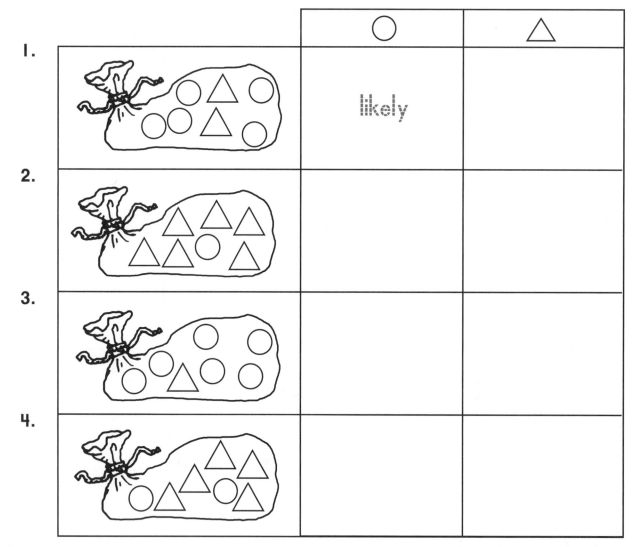

	○	△
1.	likely	
2.		
3.		
4.		

 Mixed Review

Use the calendar to answer
the question.

5. What is the date of
the second Sunday?

_____

MARCH						
Sunday	Monday	Tuesday	Wednesday	Thursday	Friday	Saturday
	1	2	3	4	5	6
7	8	9	10	11	12	13
14	15	16	17	18	19	20
21	22	23	24	25	26	27
28	29	30	31			

Name _____

Likelihood of Events

Draw to show which shape belongs in each column.

		Most Likely	Least Likely
1.			
2.			
3.			
4.			

5. Circle the bag from which pulling a square is most likely.

6. Mark an X on the bag from which pulling a triangle is least likely.

▶ Mixed Review

About how long will it take? Circle the better estimate.

7. to walk to a friend's house   5 minutes   5 hours

8. to do homework   3 minutes   30 minutes

9. to make your bed   5 minutes   5 hours

Name _____

Equally Likely

Draw to show which shapes are equally likely to
be pulled from the bag. Then answer the question.

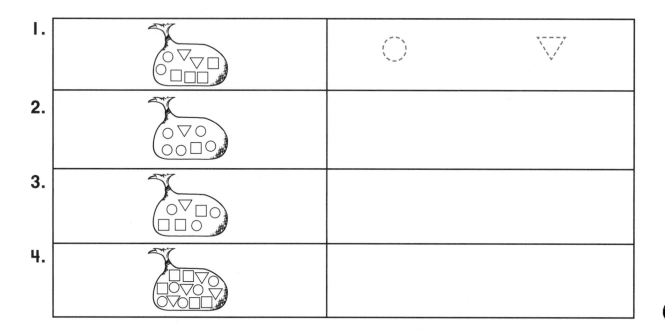

5. A bag has 4 circles, 4 squares, and 2 triangles.
Which shapes are equally likely to be pulled?

_____

▶ **Mixed Review**

Write the months in order.

6. October, March, September, May

_____

7. November, April, February, July

_____

LESSON 17.6

LESSON 17.6

Problem Solving • Use a Table

Use the table to answer the question.

1. Liz put some buttons in a box. She recorded the outcomes of 20 pulls to see which color was less likely to be pulled.

   Which color did Liz pull less often?

   _____white_____

Pulls of Buttons from the Box	
Color	**Tally**
black	ЖHT ЖHT II
white	ЖHT III

2. Miles had a bag of animal crackers. He recorded the outcomes of 30 pulls to see which animal was least likely to be pulled.

   Which animal did Miles pull least often?

   _____

Pulls of Crackers from the Bag	
Animal	**Tally**
elephant	ЖHT ЖHT ЖHT
lion	ЖHT I
bear	ЖHT IIII

3. Ada pulled some shapes from a bin. She recorded the outcomes of 10 pulls to see which shape was most likely to be pulled.

pull	1	2	3	4	5	6	7	8	9	10
shape	○	△	□	△	△	□	△	○	△	□

   Which shape did Ada pull most often?

   _____

Plane Shapes

Follow the directions.

1. Color the rectangles orange.

2. Color the circles blue.

3. Color the hexagons yellow.

4. Color the triangles red.

5. Color the squares green.

6. Color the circles yellow.

7. Color the trapezoids red.

8. Color the hexagons green.

9. Color the parallelogram blue.

10. Color the triangles orange.

 **Mixed Review**

Subtract.

11. $43 - 5 =$ _____ $33 - 5 =$ _____ $18 - 5 =$ _____

12. $27 - 5 =$ _____ $41 - 5 =$ _____ $94 - 5 =$ _____

13. $45 - 5 =$ _____ $64 - 5 =$ _____ $70 - 5 =$ _____

Algebra: Sort Plane Shapes

Write a title for each group of plane shapes.

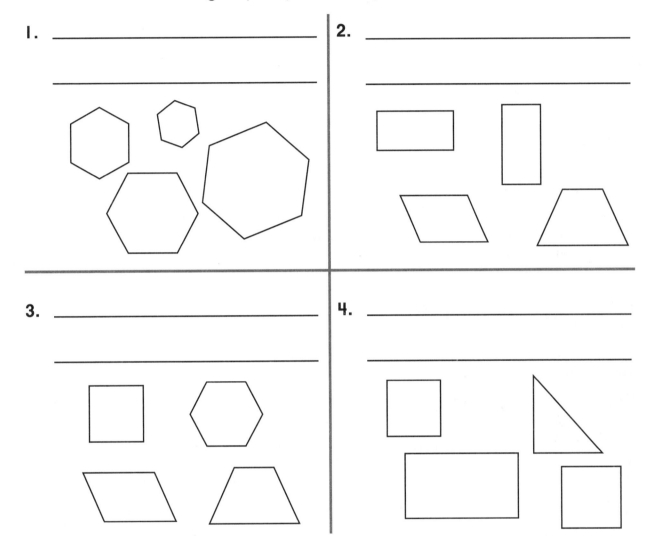

1. _____

   _____

2. _____

   _____

3. _____

   _____

4. _____

   _____

▶ **Mixed Review**

Write **likely** or **unlikely** to tell the chance of pulling a white square and a gray square from the bag.

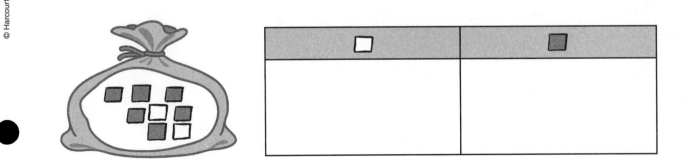

Combine and Separate Shapes

Place pattern blocks on top of the shape. Draw lines inside the
shape to show what shapes you put together.

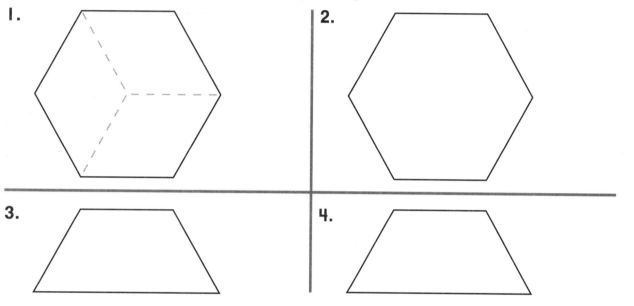

1.

2.

3.

4.

▶ **Mixed Review**

Follow the directions.

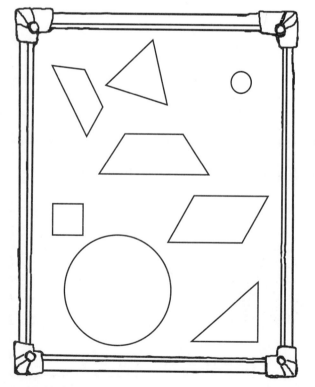

5. Color the triangles green.

6. Color the circles yellow.

7. Color the squares blue.

8. Color the trapezoids red.

9. Color the parallelograms
   orange.

Problem Solving • Make a Model

Use pattern blocks. Make and draw a model to solve.

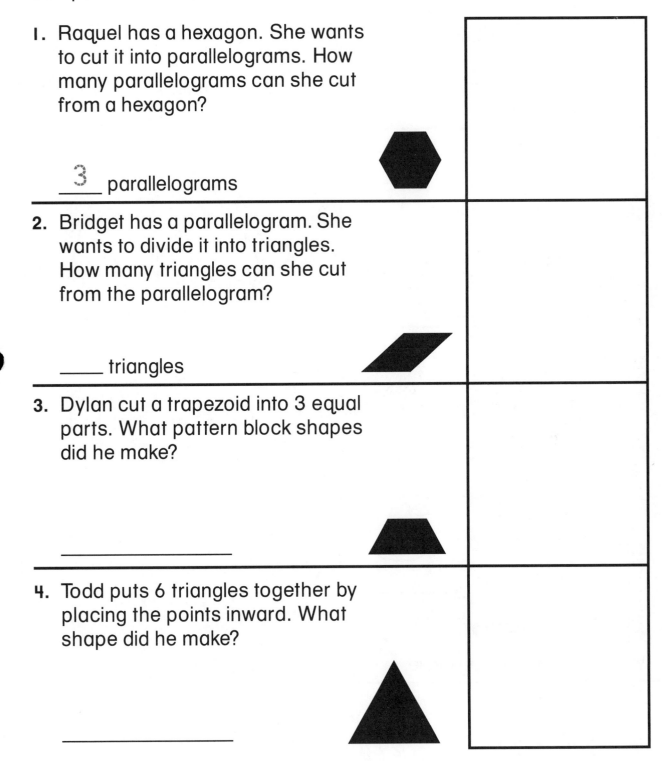

1. Raquel has a hexagon. She wants to cut it into parallelograms. How many parallelograms can she cut from a hexagon?

   __3__ parallelograms

2. Bridget has a parallelogram. She wants to divide it into triangles. How many triangles can she cut from the parallelogram?

   _____ triangles

3. Dylan cut a trapezoid into 3 equal parts. What pattern block shapes did he make?

   _____

4. Todd puts 6 triangles together by placing the points inward. What shape did he make?

   _____

Solid Figures

rectangular prisms   sphere   cones   cylinders   cubes   pyramids

Color the figures that are the same shape.

1.

2.

3.

4.

5.

6.

▶ **Mixed Review**

Write >, <, or = in the circle.

7. 44 ◯ 54   82 ◯ 28   21 ◯ 21

8. 77 ◯ 77   29 ◯ 92   41 ◯ 14

9. 10 ◯ 7   33 ◯ 31   19 ◯ 19

Name _____

Algebra: Sort Solid Figures

Complete the table. Write how many.

Number of Faces, Edges, and Vertices			
solid figure	faces	edges	vertices
1. rectangular prism	6	_____	_____
2. pyramid	_____	_____	_____
3. cube	_____	_____	_____
4. sphere	_____	_____	_____

▶ **Mixed Review**

Count on to find the total amount.

5.

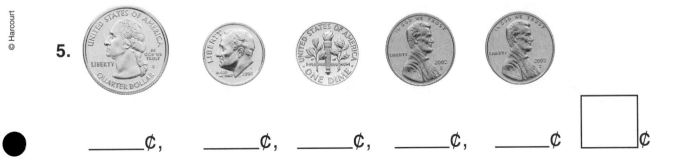

_____ ¢, _____ ¢, _____ ¢, _____ ¢, _____ ¢ ☐ ¢

Practice PW103

Compare Solid Figures and Plane Shapes

Use solid figures. Look at the faces.
Circle the solid figure you can make from the shapes.

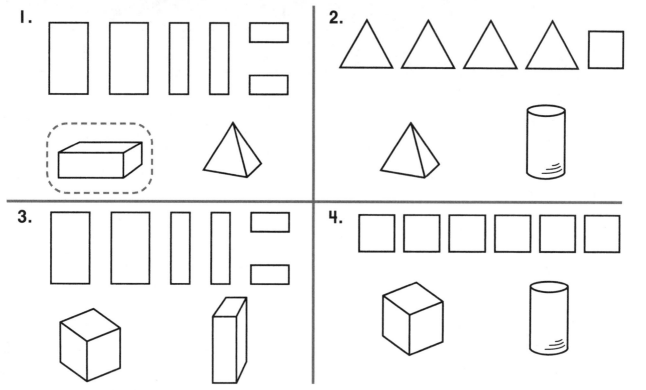

▶ **Mixed Review**

Subtract.

5.	6.	7.	8.	9.
27 − 8	54 − 9	37 − 8	32 − 6	51 − 7

10.	11.	12.	13.	14.
63 − 8	44 − 5	86 − 8	95 − 7	24 − 4

© Harcourt

Problem Solving • Make a Table

Complete the table and solve.

1. Jacob is making three solid figures. He plans to make 2 cubes and one pyramid. How many of each plane shape does he need to make the faces of the three figures?

Number of Shapes Needed for Solid Figures		
solid figure	squares	triangles
cube	6	0
total		

Jacob needs _____ squares and _____ triangles.

2. Shannon is making four solid figures. She plans to make two rectangular prisms and two cubes. How many of each plane shape does she need to make the faces of the four figures?

Number of Shapes Needed for Solid Figures		
solid figure	rectangles	squares
rectangular prism	6	0
total		

Shannon needs _____ rectangles and _____ squares.

Congruence

Are the two figures congruent?
Circle **Yes** or **No**.

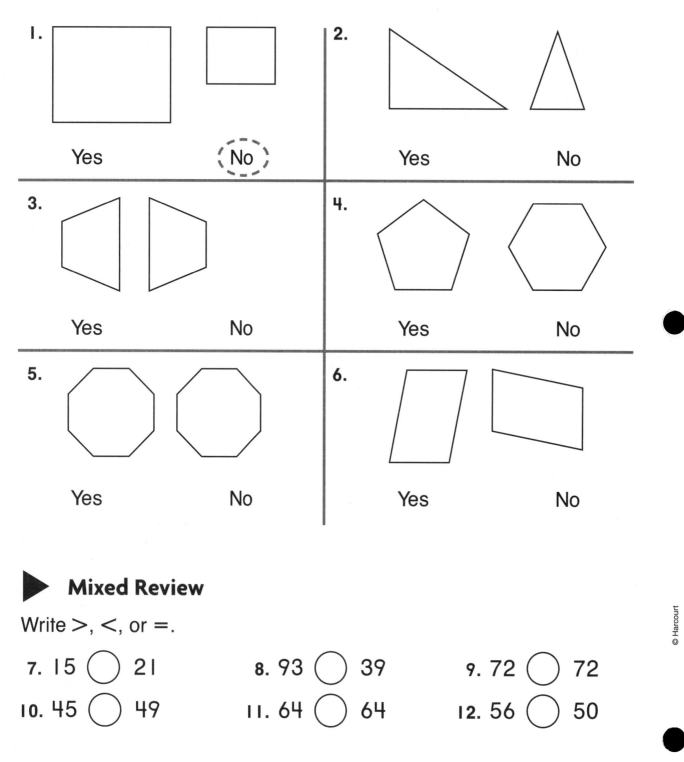

1.

Yes   (No)

2.

Yes   No

3.

Yes   No

4.

Yes   No

5.

Yes   No

6.

Yes   No

▶ **Mixed Review**

Write >, <, or =.

7. 15 ◯ 21   8. 93 ◯ 39   9. 72 ◯ 72

10. 45 ◯ 49   11. 64 ◯ 64   12. 56 ◯ 50

© Harcourt

Symmetry

Draw a line of symmetry.
The two parts will be congruent.

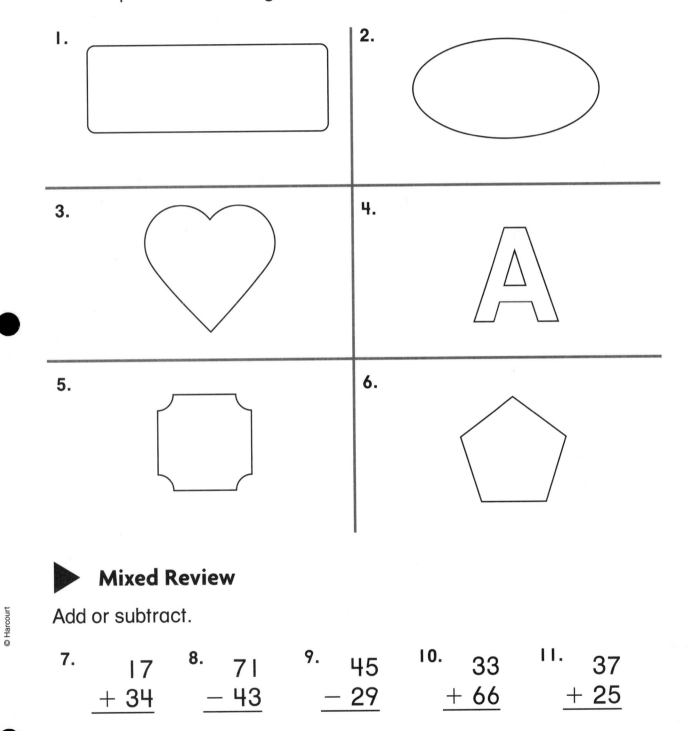

1.

2.

3.

4.

5.

6.

▶ **Mixed Review**

Add or subtract.

7. $\begin{array}{r} 17 \\ + 34 \\ \hline \end{array}$
8. $\begin{array}{r} 71 \\ - 43 \\ \hline \end{array}$
9. $\begin{array}{r} 45 \\ - 29 \\ \hline \end{array}$
10. $\begin{array}{r} 33 \\ + 66 \\ \hline \end{array}$
11. $\begin{array}{r} 37 \\ + 25 \\ \hline \end{array}$

Slides, Flips, and Turns

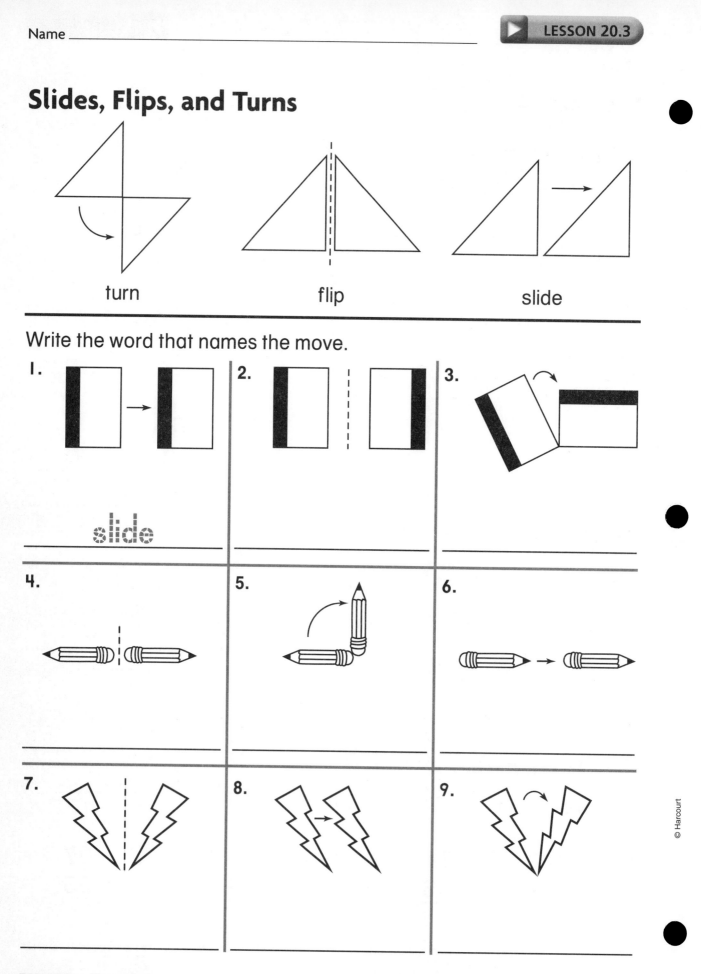

turn   flip   slide

Write the word that names the move.

1.

___slide___

2.

_____

3.

_____

4.

_____

5.

_____

6.

_____

7.

_____

8.

_____

9.

_____

© Harcourt

Name _____

Problem Solving • Predict and Test

Predict which figure will show the reflection. Underline it.
Then place your mirror on the dashed line to test. Circle
the letter of the correct figure.

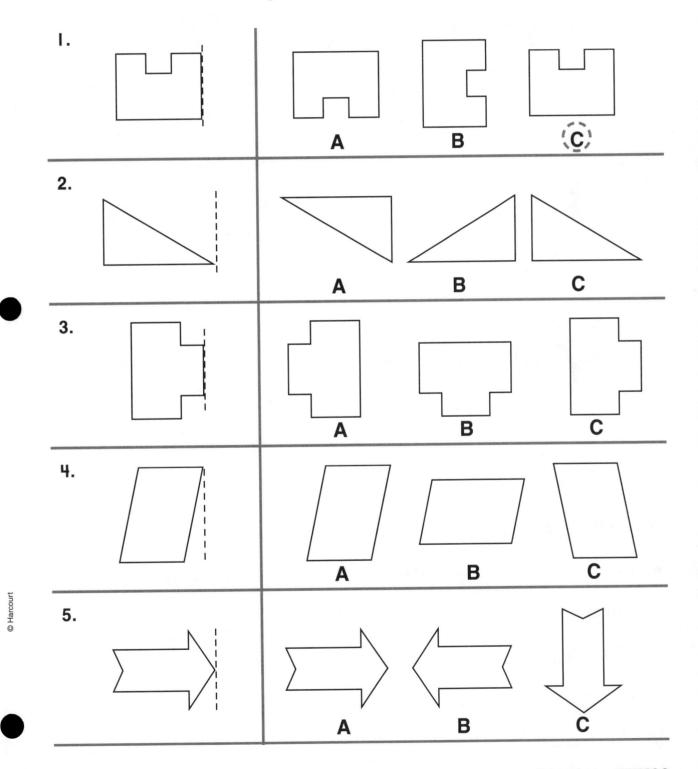

Algebra: Describe Patterns

Describe the pattern.
Circle the pattern unit.

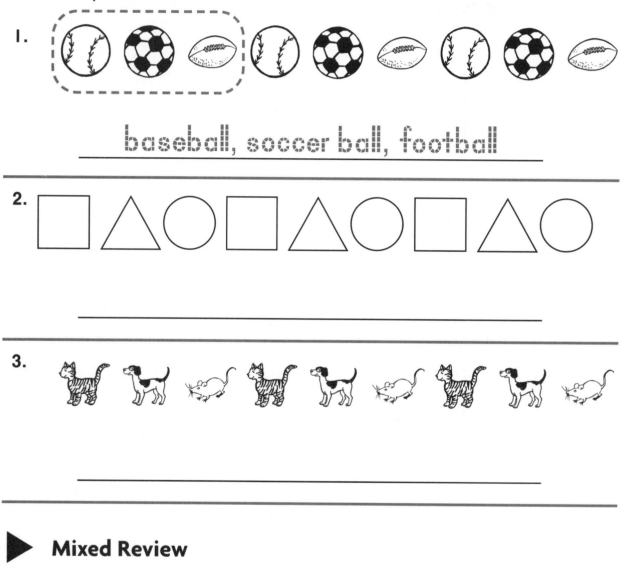

1. _____baseball, soccer ball, football_____

2.

3.

▶ **Mixed Review**

Write the missing day or month.

4. Tuesday, _____, Thursday

5. February, _____, April

6. Sunday, Monday, _____, Wednesday

7. July, _____, September

Name _____

Algebra: Extend Pattern Units

Draw and color to extend the pattern.

1.

2.

3.

▶ **Mixed Review**

Use the spinner to answer the questions.

4. Which number are you
   least likely to spin? _____

5. Which number are you
   most likely to spin? _____

6. Are you more likely to
   spin a 2 or a 6? _____

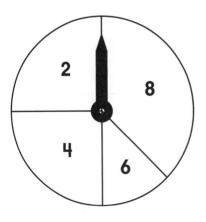

Algebra: Make Patterns

1. Choose three pattern blocks to make a pattern unit.
   Draw the pattern. Repeat three times.

2. Use the same three pattern blocks to make
   a different pattern unit. Draw the pattern.

3. Use the same three pattern blocks to make
   a different pattern unit. Draw the pattern.

▶ **Mixed Review**

Write the missing number.

4. 8, 10, 12, _____, 16, 18

5. 15, 20, _____, 30, 35, 40

6. _____, 40, 50, 60, 70

7. 18, 20, 22, 24, _____, 28

Name _____

Problem Solving • Transfer a Pattern

Show the pattern another way.

1. Li made a pattern with beads.

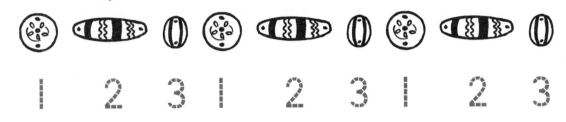

2. Ryan made a pattern with shapes.

3. Anna made a pattern with shells.

4. Tim made a pattern with stars

© Harcourt

Problem Solving • Correct a Pattern

Read the pattern. Circle the mistake. Correct the pattern.

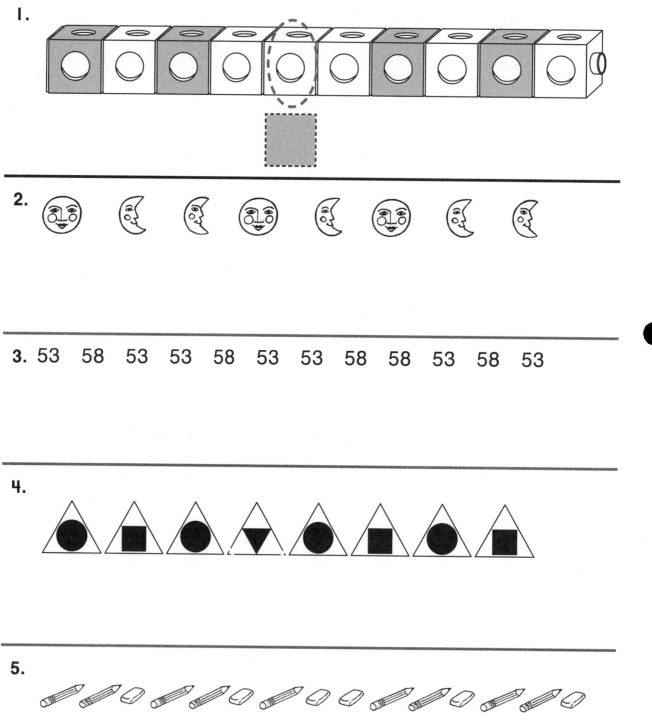

1.

2.

3. 53   58   53   53   58   53   53   58   58   53   58   53

4.

5.

Name _____

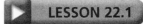

Measure Length with Nonstandard Units

Measure each real object with paper clips or footsteps.

1.

about _____ paper clips

2.

about _____ footsteps

3.

about _____ footsteps

4.

about _____ paper clips

▶ **Mixed Review**

Add or subtract.

5.

12	27	35	42	21
+ 9	+ 5	− 7	− 9	+12

6.

58	62	43	64	72
−23	−10	+21	+31	−41

Length and Distance

Measure the paths with string.
Cut the strings and compare the lengths.
Write 1, 2, and 3 to show the order from shortest to longest.

Your desk to the window	Your desk to the chalkboard	Your desk to the door
_____	_____	_____

Circle the correct answer to the question.

1. Which path is longer?
 	
    1   2
	2. Which path is longer?
	
	    2 3

3. Which path is shorter?
 	
    1   3
	4. Which path is shorter?
	
	    2 3

5. Which path is shortest?
 	
    1   2   3
	6. Which path is longest?
	
	    1 2 3

▶ **Mixed Review**

Write the number of faces on each solid figure.

7.

    _____

8.

    _____

9.

    _____

Name _____

Measure to the Nearest Inch

Work with a partner. Estimate.
Then measure to the nearest inch.

1. crayon

Estimate: about _____ inches
Measure: about _____ inches

2. book

Estimate: about _____ inches
Measure: about _____ inches

3. pencil

Estimate: about _____ inches
Measure: about _____ inches

4. tape dispenser

Estimate: about _____ inches
Measure: about _____ inches

5. stapler

Estimate: about _____ inches
Measure: about _____ inches

6. sheet of paper

Estimate: about _____ inches
Measure: about _____ inches

▶ **Mixed Review**

Draw a line of symmetry.

7.

8.

9.

10.

11.

12.

© Harcourt

Inch, Foot, and Yard

Choose the best unit of measure.
Write your measurement to the nearest inch, foot, or yard.

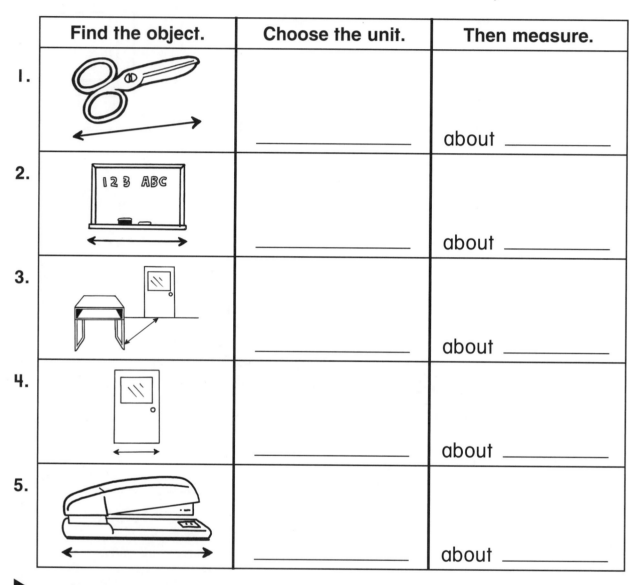

	Find the object.	Choose the unit.	Then measure.
1.		_____	about _____
2.	1 2 3 ABC	_____	about _____
3.		_____	about _____
4.		_____	about _____
5.		_____	about _____

▶ **Mixed Review**

Circle the two figures that are congruent.

6. ○ □ ◯ □ | 7. △ ◯ ○ △

Name _____

Fahrenheit Thermometer

Read the thermometer. Write the temperature.

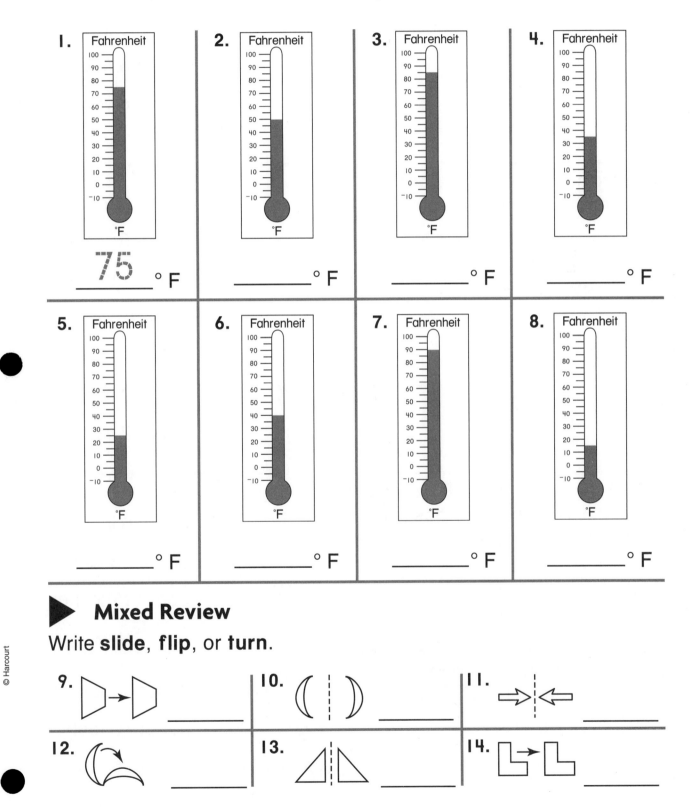

1. Fahrenheit

__75__ ° F

2. Fahrenheit

_____ ° F

3. Fahrenheit

_____ ° F

4. Fahrenheit

_____ ° F

5. Fahrenheit

_____ ° F

6. Fahrenheit

_____ ° F

7. Fahrenheit

_____ ° F

8. Fahrenheit

_____ ° F

▶ **Mixed Review**

Write **slide**, **flip**, or **turn**.

9. _____

10. _____

11. _____

12. _____

13. _____

14. _____

Problem Solving • Make Reasonable Estimates

Circle the reasonable estimate.

1. Bill is resting on the couch.
   About how long is the couch?

   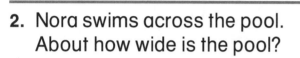

   about 6 inches

   about 6 feet

   about 6 yards

2. Nora swims across the pool.
   About how wide is the pool?

   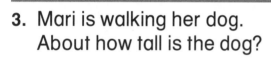

   about 2 feet

   about 5 yards

   about 11 inches

3. Mari is walking her dog.
   About how tall is the dog?

   about 2 inches

   about 2 feet

   about 2 yards

4. Tina's bean plant is 10 inches tall.
   Last week it was 8 inches tall.
   About how tall will it be next week?

   about 5 inches

   about 13 inches

   about 19 inches

5. Jacy is riding his bicycle.
   About how long is the bicycle?

   about 5 feet

   about 10 feet

   about 15 feet

Measure Capacity with

Units of Measure	
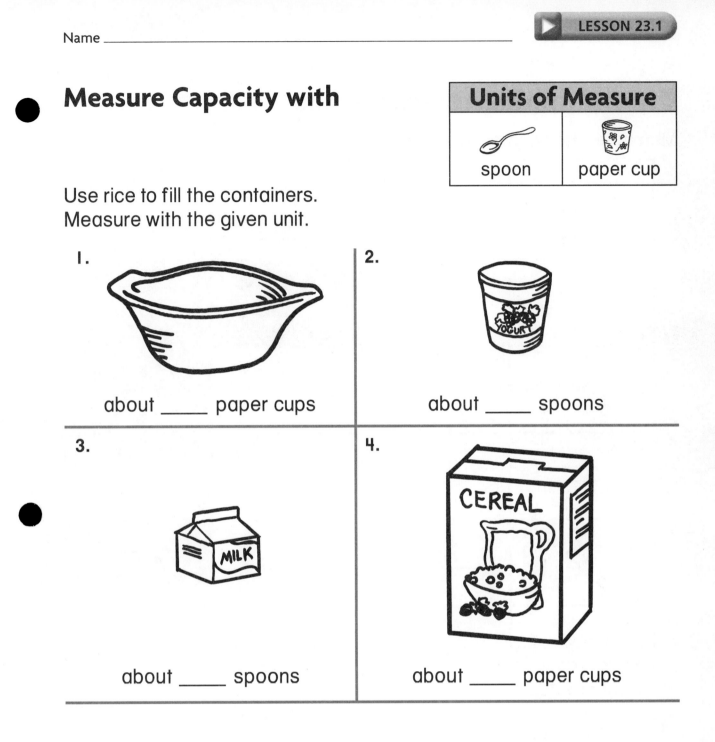 spoon	paper cup

Use rice to fill the containers.
Measure with the given unit.

1.

about _____ paper cups

2.

about _____ spoons

3.

about _____ spoons

4.

about _____ paper cups

▶ **Mixed Review**

Choose the best unit of measure. Write **inch, foot,** or **yard**.

5.

6.

7.

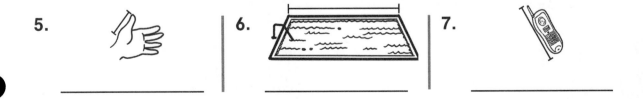

_____   _____   _____

Cups, Pints, Quarts, and Gallons

Measure. Then complete the chart.

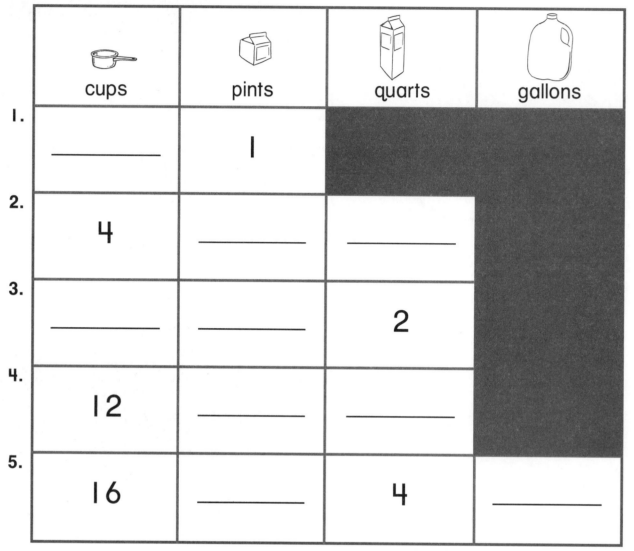

	cups	pints	quarts	gallons
1.	_____	1		
2.	4	_____	_____	
3.	_____	_____	2	
4.	12	_____	_____	
5.	16	_____	4	_____

▶ **Mixed Review**

Write the number of vertices on each solid figure.

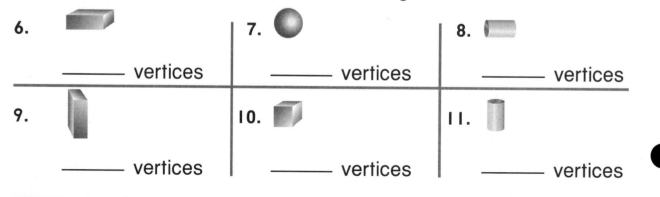

6. _____ vertices

7. _____ vertices

8. _____ vertices

9. _____ vertices

10. _____ vertices

11. _____ vertices

Name _____

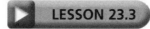

Measure Weight with Nonstandard Units

Estimate. Then weigh the object.
Measure with the given unit.

1. 🔟 dime

Estimate: about _____ paper clips

Measure: about _____ paper clips

2. scissors

Estimate: about _____ cubes

Measure: about _____ cubes

3. pencil

Estimate: about _____ cubes

Measure: about _____ cubes

4. pen cap

Estimate: about _____ paper clips

Measure: about _____ paper clips

▶ **Mixed Review**

Measure each worm to the nearest inch.

5. about _____ inches

6. about _____ inches

7. about _____ inches

© Harcourt

Ounces and Pounds

How much does the object weigh?
Estimate. Then measure.

THINK:
The grapes weigh a little more than 2 pounds. So, 2 is the nearest pound.

	object	estimate	measurement
1.	clock	about _____ pounds	about _____ pounds
2.	book	about _____ pounds	about _____ pounds
3.	soccer ball	about _____ pounds	about _____ pounds
4.	pitcher	about _____ pounds	about _____ pounds
5.	trash can	about _____ pounds	about _____ pounds

▶ **Mixed Review**

Circle the greater length.

6. 8 inches   I foot

7. 2 feet   I yard

8. 13 inches   I foot

9. 10 inches   2 yards

10. 3 feet   15 inches

11. 4 feet   2 yards

Problem Solving • Choose the Measuring Tool

Measure a paper cup in different ways.
Then complete the chart.

	what to measure	tool	measurement
1.	the cup's length	_____	about ____ inches
2.	the cup's weight	_____	about ____ pounds
3.	how much the cup holds	_____	about ____ cups
4.	the temperature of the water	_____	about ____ °F

Measure a pitcher in different ways.
Then complete the chart.

	what to measure	tool	measurement
5.	the pitcher's length	_____	about ____ inches
6.	the pitcher's weight	_____	about ____ pounds
7.	how much the pitcher holds	_____	about ____ cups
8.	the temperature of the water	_____	about ____ °F

Centimeters and Meters

Estimate the length.
Then measure to the nearest centimeter.

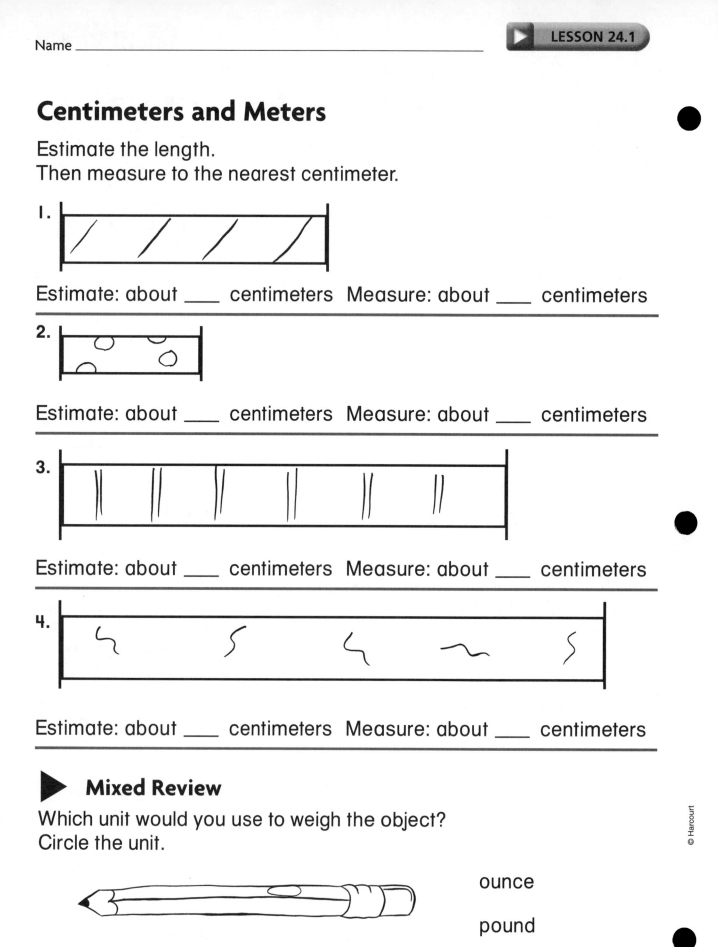

1.

Estimate: about ___ centimeters   Measure: about ___ centimeters

2.

Estimate: about ___ centimeters   Measure: about ___ centimeters

3.

Estimate: about ___ centimeters   Measure: about ___ centimeters

4.

Estimate: about ___ centimeters   Measure: about ___ centimeters

▶ **Mixed Review**

Which unit would you use to weigh the object?
Circle the unit.

ounce

pound

© Harcourt

Milliliters and Liters

How many 🍶 does the container hold?
Estimate. Then measure.

	Object	Estimate	Measurement
1.	jar	about _____ liters	about _____ liters
2.	waste basket	about _____ liters	about _____ liters
3.	pitcher	about _____ liters	about _____ liters
4.	teapot	about _____ liters	about _____ liters
5.	watering can	about _____ liters	about _____ liters

► **Mixed Review**

Solve.

6. $\begin{array}{r} 25 \\ +7 \\ \hline \end{array}$	7. $\begin{array}{r} 33 \\ +29 \\ \hline \end{array}$	8. $\begin{array}{r} 88 \\ +3 \\ \hline \end{array}$	9. $\begin{array}{r} 16 \\ +36 \\ \hline \end{array}$	10. $\begin{array}{r} 25 \\ +7 \\ \hline \end{array}$

Grams and Kilograms

What is the mass of the object?
Estimate. Then measure.

Object	Estimate	Measurement
1. book	about ____ kilograms	about ____ kilograms
2. computer	about ____ kilograms	about ____ kilograms
3. shoes	about ____ kilograms	about ____ kilograms
4. lunch box	about ____ kilograms	about ____ kilograms
5. bicycle	about ____ kilograms	about ____ kilograms

▶ **Mixed Review**

Subtract.

6.
$$\begin{array}{r} 78 \\ -19 \\ \hline \end{array}$$
$$\begin{array}{r} 38 \\ -25 \\ \hline \end{array}$$
$$\begin{array}{r} 73 \\ -12 \\ \hline \end{array}$$
$$\begin{array}{r} 82 \\ -44 \\ \hline \end{array}$$
$$\begin{array}{r} 25 \\ -18 \\ \hline \end{array}$$

© Harcourt

Celsius Thermometer

Circle the better estimate.

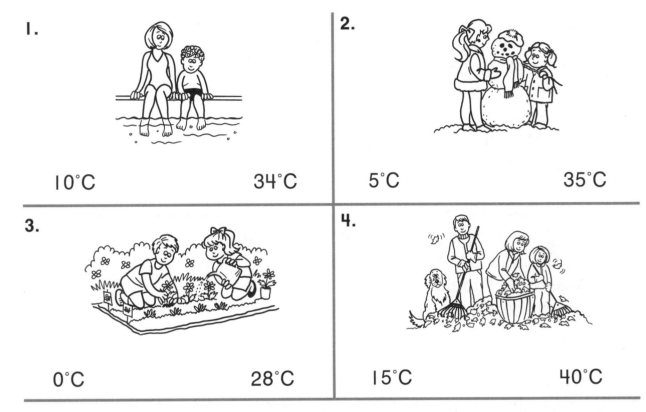

1.

10°C   34°C

2.

5°C   35°C

3.

0°C   28°C

4.

15°C   40°C

▶ **Mixed Review**

Write the amount.

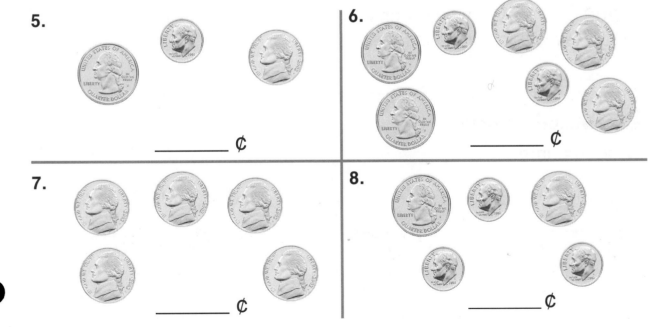

5.

_____ ¢

6.

_____ ¢

7.

_____ ¢

8.

_____ ¢

Problem Solving • Use Logical Reasoning

Use logical reasoning to solve the problem.
Draw a picture to solve.

1. Pat puts toys into three boxes. The boxes
   are red, yellow, and blue. The red box
   holds the greatest number of toys. The
   blue box does not hold the least number
   of toys. Which box holds the least
   number of toys?

   _____

2. Dylan puts three objects in order by length.
   The shoelace is the shortest. The belt is
   between the shoelace and the tie. Which
   object is the longest?

   _____

3. Juan weighs three apples. The apples are
   red, green, and yellow. They weigh about
   200 grams, 180 grams, and 220 grams.
   The red apple has a mass of about
   200 grams. The yellow apple is not the
   lightest. Which apple is the lightest?

   _____

▶ **Mixed Review**

Write the time.

4.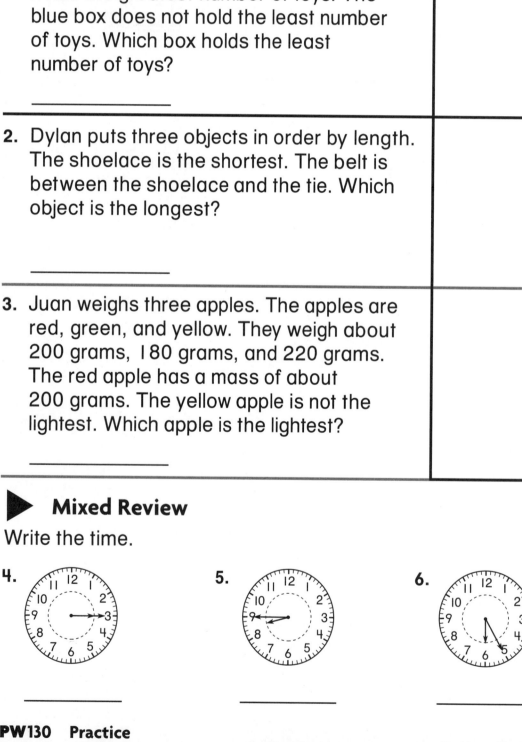

   _____

5.

   _____

6.

   _____

Perimeter

Use a centimeter ruler to measure each side.
Add to find the perimeter.

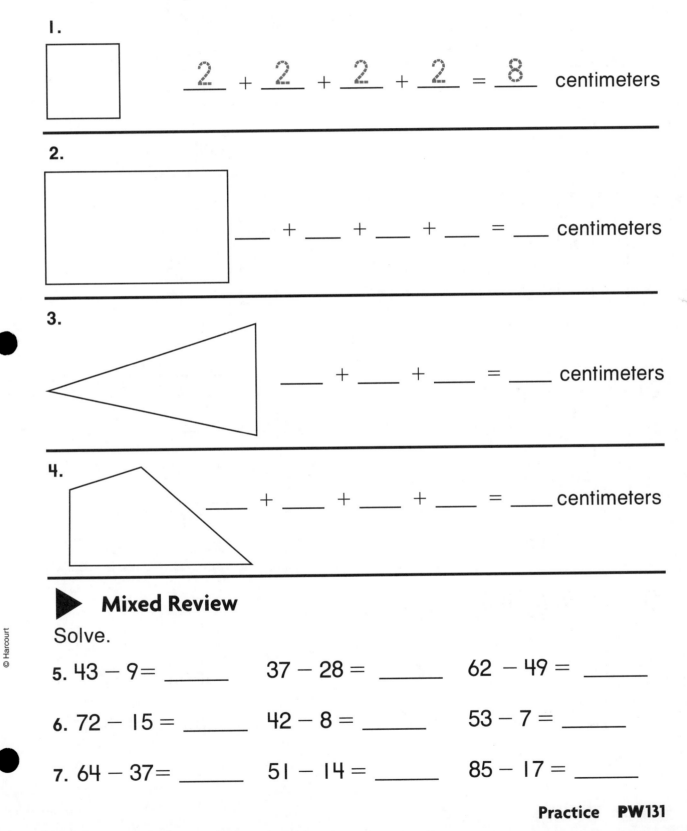

1.

_2_ + _2_ + _2_ + _2_ = _8_ centimeters

2.

___ + ___ + ___ + ___ = ___ centimeters

3.

___ + ___ + ___ = ___ centimeters

4.

___ + ___ + ___ + ___ = ___ centimeters

▶ **Mixed Review**

Solve.

5. $43 - 9 =$ _____ $37 - 28 =$ _____ $62 - 49 =$ _____

6. $72 - 15 =$ _____ $42 - 8 =$ _____ $53 - 7 =$ _____

7. $64 - 37 =$ _____ $51 - 14 =$ _____ $85 - 17 =$ _____

Area

Find the area of each figure.

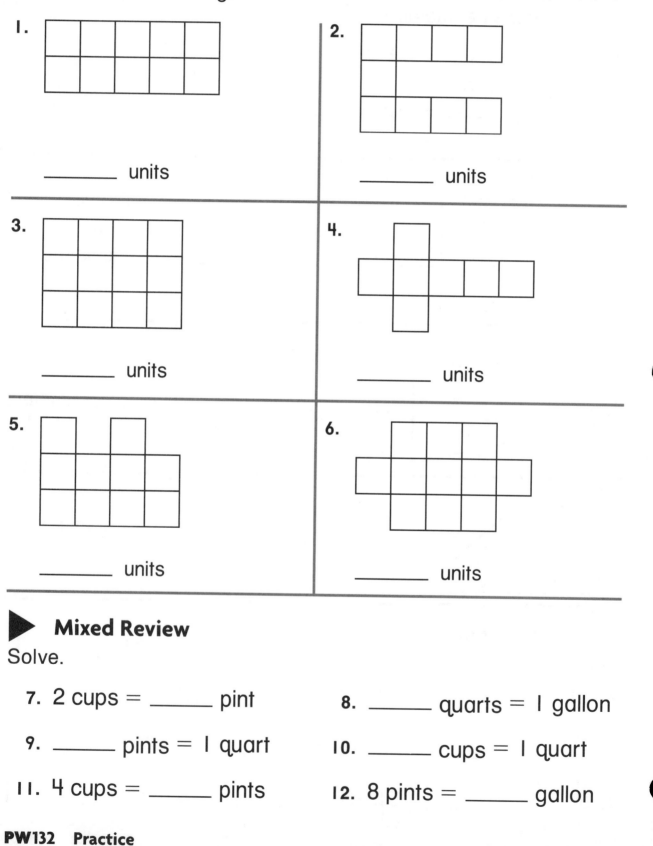

1.

_____ units

2.

_____ units

3.

_____ units

4.

_____ units

5.

_____ units

6.

_____ units

▶ **Mixed Review**

Solve.

7. 2 cups = _____ pint

8. _____ quarts = 1 gallon

9. _____ pints = 1 quart

10. _____ cups = 1 quart

11. 4 cups = _____ pints

12. 8 pints = _____ gallon

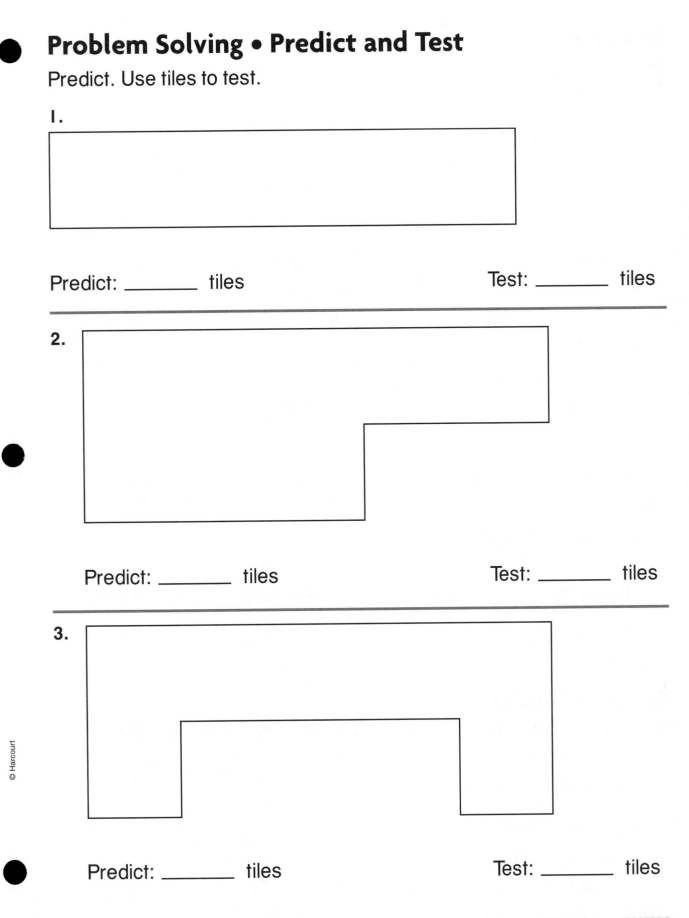

Problem Solving • Predict and Test

Predict. Use tiles to test.

1.

Predict: _____ tiles   Test: _____ tiles

2.

Predict: _____ tiles   Test: _____ tiles

3.

Predict: _____ tiles   Test: _____ tiles

© Harcourt

Volume

Estimate the volume.
Then count to find the volume.

1.

Estimate: _____ cubes

Count: _____ cubes

2.

Estimate: _____ cubes

Count: _____ cubes

3.

Estimate: _____ cubes

Count: _____ cubes

4.

Estimate: _____ cubes

Count: _____ cubes

5.

Estimate: _____ cubes

Count: _____ cubes

6.

Estimate: _____ cubes

Count: _____ cubes

▶ **Mixed Review**

Choose the best unit of measure. Write **meter**, **gram**, or **liter**.

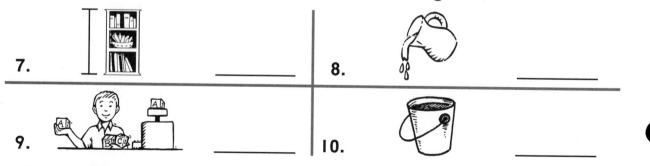

7. _____

8. _____

9. _____

10. _____

Name _____

Unit Fractions

Draw lines to show equal parts. Shade one part.
Write the fraction for the shaded part.

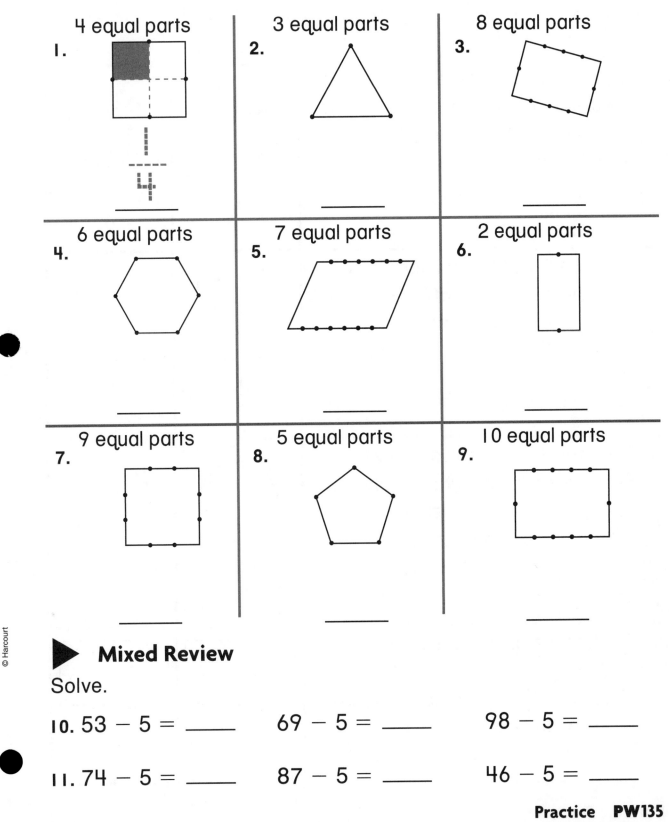

4 equal parts

1.

$\dfrac{1}{4}$

3 equal parts

2.

_____

8 equal parts

3.

_____

6 equal parts

4.

_____

7 equal parts

5.

_____

2 equal parts

6.

_____

9 equal parts

7.

_____

5 equal parts

8.

_____

10 equal parts

9.

_____

▶ **Mixed Review**

Solve.

10. $53 - 5 =$ _____ $69 - 5 =$ _____ $98 - 5 =$ _____

11. $74 - 5 =$ _____ $87 - 5 =$ _____ $46 - 5 =$ _____

Problem Solving • Make a Model

Use fraction bars or fraction circles.
Color one part of each whole.
Circle the fraction that is greater.
Answer the question.

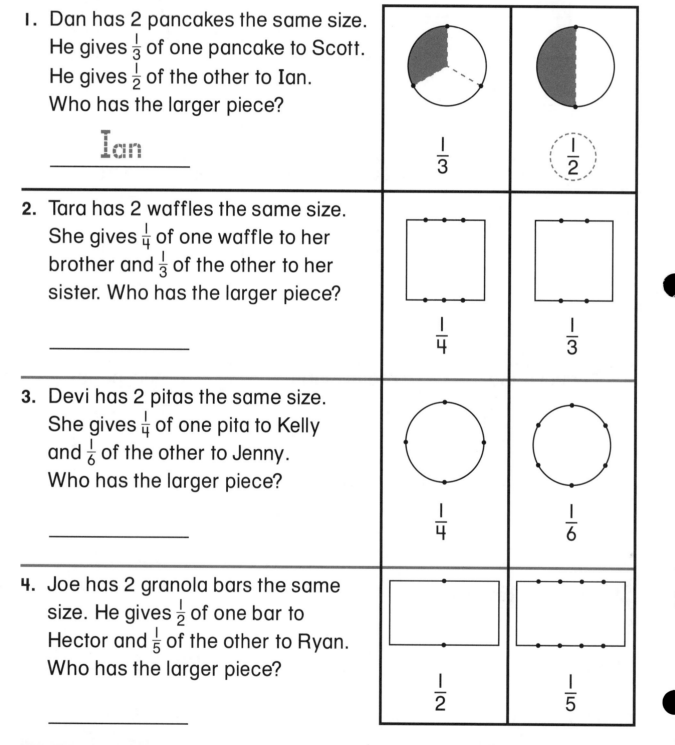

1. Dan has 2 pancakes the same size.
   He gives $\frac{1}{3}$ of one pancake to Scott.
   He gives $\frac{1}{2}$ of the other to Ian.
   Who has the larger piece?

   __Ian__

   $\frac{1}{3}$ $\frac{1}{2}$

2. Tara has 2 waffles the same size.
   She gives $\frac{1}{4}$ of one waffle to her
   brother and $\frac{1}{3}$ of the other to her
   sister. Who has the larger piece?

   _____

   $\frac{1}{4}$ $\frac{1}{3}$

3. Devi has 2 pitas the same size.
   She gives $\frac{1}{4}$ of one pita to Kelly
   and $\frac{1}{6}$ of the other to Jenny.
   Who has the larger piece?

   _____

   $\frac{1}{4}$ $\frac{1}{6}$

4. Joe has 2 granola bars the same
   size. He gives $\frac{1}{2}$ of one bar to
   Hector and $\frac{1}{5}$ of the other to Ryan.
   Who has the larger piece?

   _____

   $\frac{1}{2}$ $\frac{1}{5}$

Name _____

Other Fractions

Write the fraction for the shaded part.

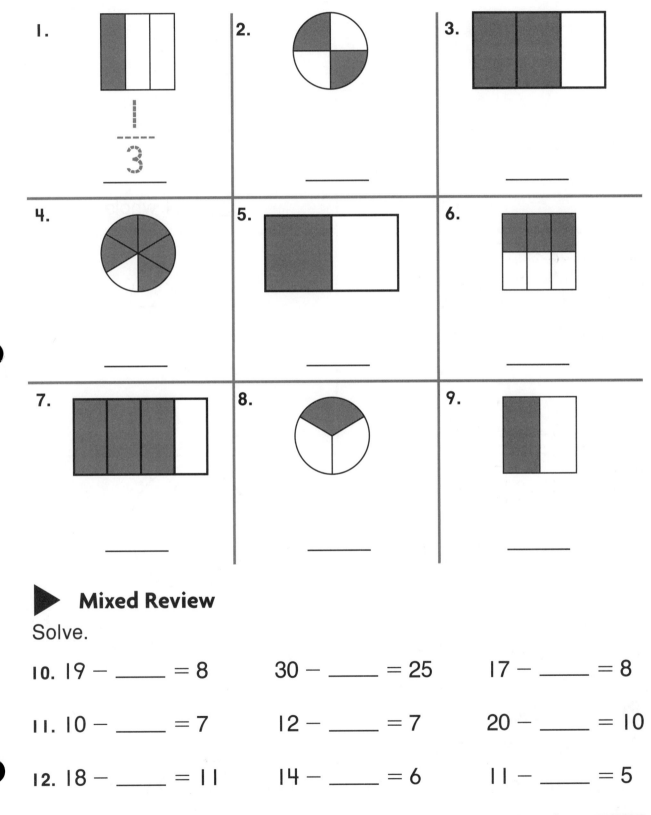

1. $\dfrac{1}{3}$

2.   _____

3.   _____

4.   _____

5.   _____

6.   _____

7.   _____

8.   _____

9.   _____

▶ **Mixed Review**

Solve.

10. $19 - \underline{\hspace{1cm}} = 8$ $30 - \underline{\hspace{1cm}} = 25$ $17 - \underline{\hspace{1cm}} = 8$

11. $10 - \underline{\hspace{1cm}} = 7$ $12 - \underline{\hspace{1cm}} = 7$ $20 - \underline{\hspace{1cm}} = 10$

12. $18 - \underline{\hspace{1cm}} = 11$ $14 - \underline{\hspace{1cm}} = 6$ $11 - \underline{\hspace{1cm}} = 5$

Fractions Equal to 1

Count the parts. Write each fraction.
Write the fraction for the whole.

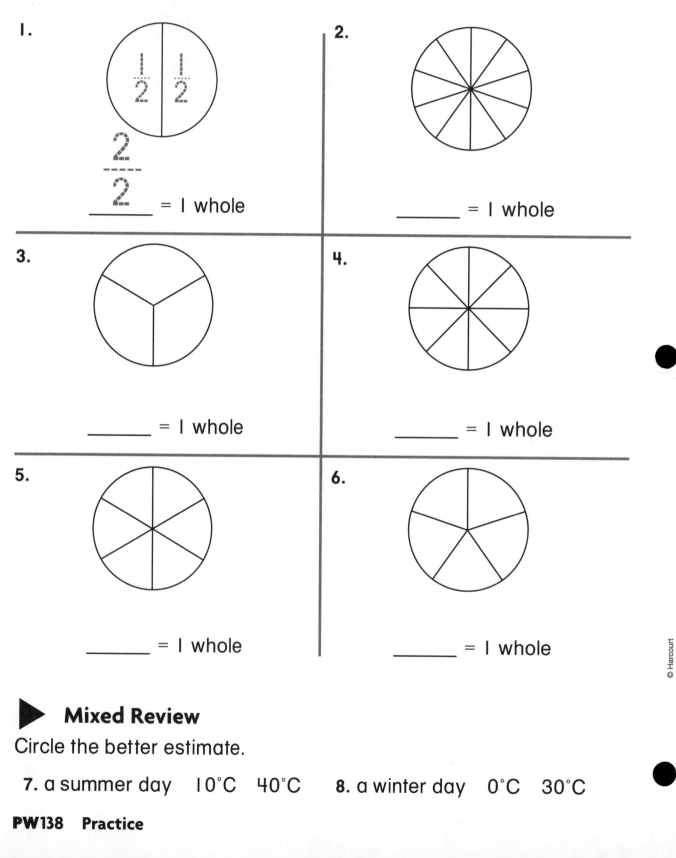

1.

$\frac{1}{2}$ $\frac{1}{2}$

$\frac{2}{2}$

_____ = I whole

2.

_____ = I whole

3.

_____ = I whole

4.

_____ = I whole

5.

_____ = I whole

6.

_____ = I whole

▶ **Mixed Review**

Circle the better estimate.

7. a summer day   10°C   40°C   **8.** a winter day   0°C   30°C

Name _____

Unit Fractions of a Group

Draw the group. Shade one part.
Write the fraction of the group for the shaded part.

1. 2 children _____	**2.** 7 cups _____
3. 5 tables _____	**4.** 9 balloons _____
5. 4 boxes _____	**6.** 3 buttons _____

▶ **Mixed Review**

Write the temperature.

7.  _____

8. 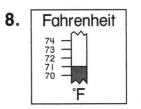 _____

Other Fractions of a Group

Toss ◯. Color these counters to show how they land.
Write the fraction of the group for each color.

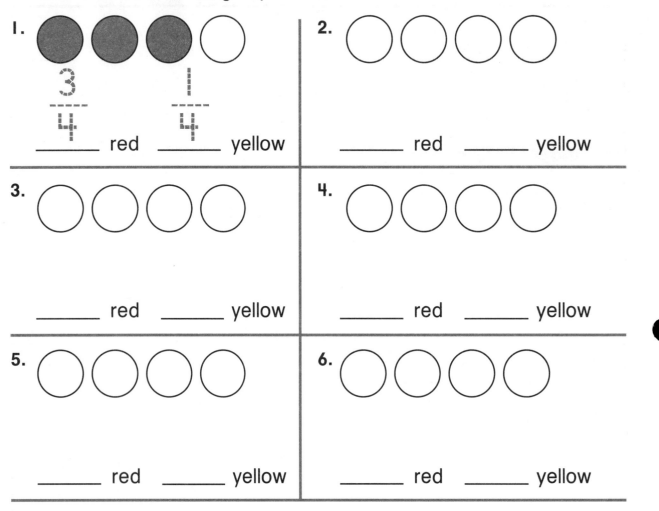

1.
$\frac{3}{4}$ _____ red $\frac{1}{4}$ _____ yellow

2.
_____ red   _____ yellow

3.
_____ red   _____ yellow

4.
_____ red   _____ yellow

5.
_____ red   _____ yellow

6.
_____ red   _____ yellow

▶ **Mixed Review**

Write **T** for True and **F** for False.

7. 16 > 61 ___   71 = 17 ___   44 > 42 ___

8. 24 < 61 ___   66 < 56 ___   88 > 18 ___

9. 9 + 9 = 18 ___   20 − 10 = 1 ___   14 − 7 = 7 ___

Hundreds

Write how many hundreds, tens, and ones.

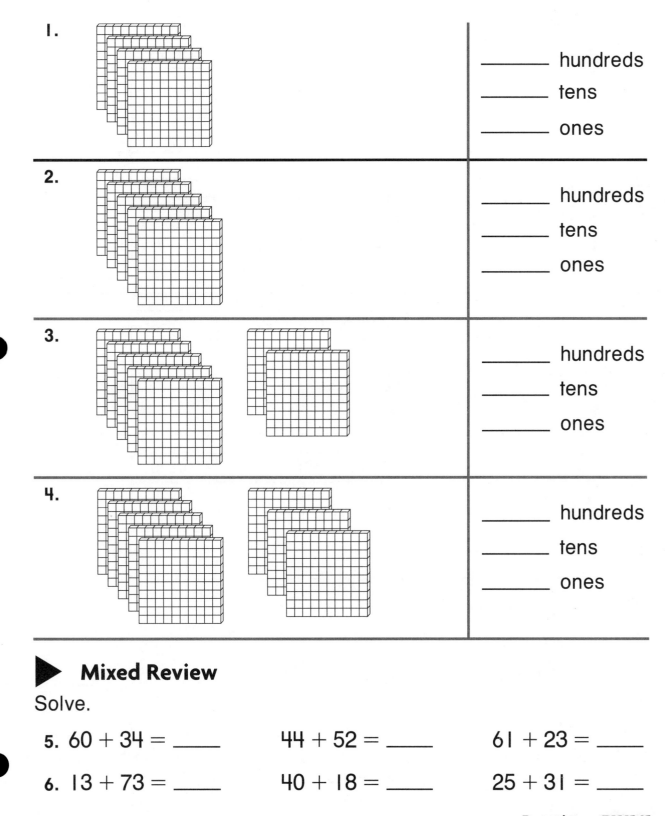

1.

_____ hundreds

_____ tens

_____ ones

2.

_____ hundreds

_____ tens

_____ ones

3.

_____ hundreds

_____ tens

_____ ones

4.

_____ hundreds

_____ tens

_____ ones

▶ **Mixed Review**

Solve.

5. $60 + 34 =$ _____ $44 + 52 =$ _____ $61 + 23 =$ _____

6. $13 + 73 =$ _____ $40 + 18 =$ _____ $25 + 31 =$ _____

Hundreds, Tens, and Ones

Write how many hundreds, tens, and ones. Then write the number.

1.

hundreds	tens	ones
4	2	6

426

2.

hundreds	tens	ones

_____

3.

hundreds	tens	ones

_____

4.

hundreds	tens	ones

_____

▶ **Mixed Review**

Add or subtract.

5. $72 - 51 =$ ___ $53 - 42 =$ ___ $66 - 50 =$ ___

6. $12 + 9 =$ ___ $15 + 7 =$ ___ $18 + 6 =$ ___

7. $57 - 24 =$ ___ $89 - 15 =$ ___ $64 - 33 =$ ___

Place Value

Circle the value of the underlined digit.

1. 3<u>6</u>4	2. <u>7</u>01	3. 25<u>9</u>
600　(60)　6	700　70　7	900　90　9
4. 54<u>8</u>	5. 4<u>6</u>3	6. 1<u>7</u>2
800　80　8	600　60　6	700　70　7
7. <u>6</u>07	8. 91<u>4</u>	9. <u>8</u>30
600　60　6	400　40　4	800　80　8
10. 52<u>6</u>	11. 1<u>8</u>1	12. <u>3</u>95
600　60　6	800　80　8	300　30　3
13. 4<u>3</u>7	14. <u>7</u>56	15. 40<u>1</u>
300　30　3	700　70　7	100　10　1

▶ **Mixed Review**

Write the missing number.

16. _____ , 52, 53　　17, _____ , 19　　63, _____ , 65

17. 34, 35, _____　　97, _____ , 99　　_____ , 84, 85

Algebra: Different Ways to Show Numbers

Circle the correct ways to show each number.
Cross out and correct the other ways.

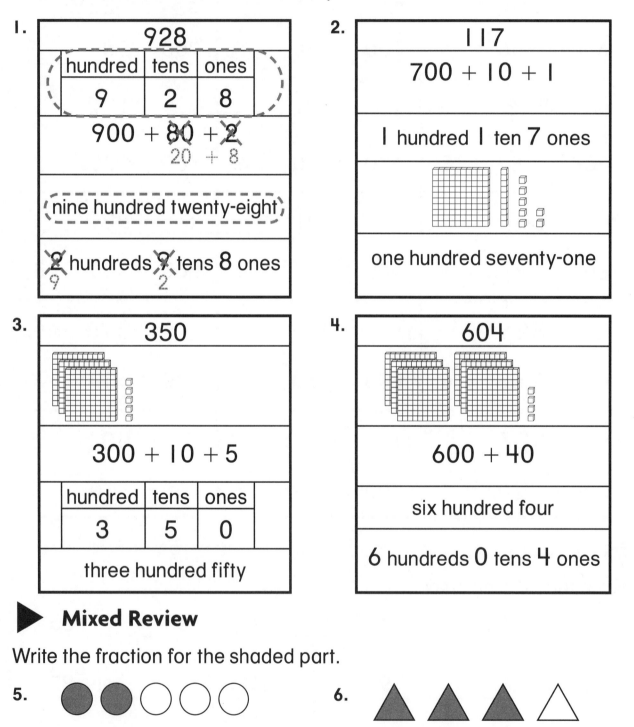

1.
928

hundred	tens	ones
9	2	8

900 + 80 + 2
~~20 + 8~~

nine hundred twenty-eight

~~2~~ hundreds ~~9~~ tens 8 ones
9   2

2.
117

700 + 10 + 1

1 hundred 1 ten 7 ones

one hundred seventy-one

3.
350

300 + 10 + 5

hundred	tens	ones
3	5	0

three hundred fifty

4.
604

600 + 40

six hundred four

6 hundreds 0 tens 4 ones

▶ **Mixed Review**

Write the fraction for the shaded part.

5. ● ● ○ ○ ○

_____

6. ▲ ▲ ▲ △

_____

© Harcourt

Problem Solving • Make a Model

Use dollar bills and coins. Count on.
Write the total amount.

1. Keb has two dollar bills,
   four dimes, and seven
   pennies. How much money
   does he have? $2.47 _____ total

2. Sean has 1 dollar bill,
   six dimes, and eight pennies.
   How much money does
   he have?   _____ total

3. Kwan has 6 dollar bills
   and five pennies. How much
   money does she have?   _____ total

4. Devi has seven dollar bills,
   seven dimes, and two pennies.
   How much money does
   she have?   _____ total

5. Beatrice has five dollar bills
   and nine dimes. How much
   money does she have?   _____ total

▶ **Mixed Review**

Find the area of the figure.

6.

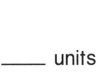 _____ units

7.

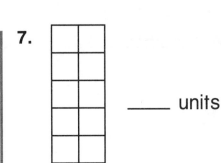 _____ units

Algebra: Compare Numbers: >, <, and =

Write **is greater than, is less than,** or **is equal to**.
Then write >, <, or =.

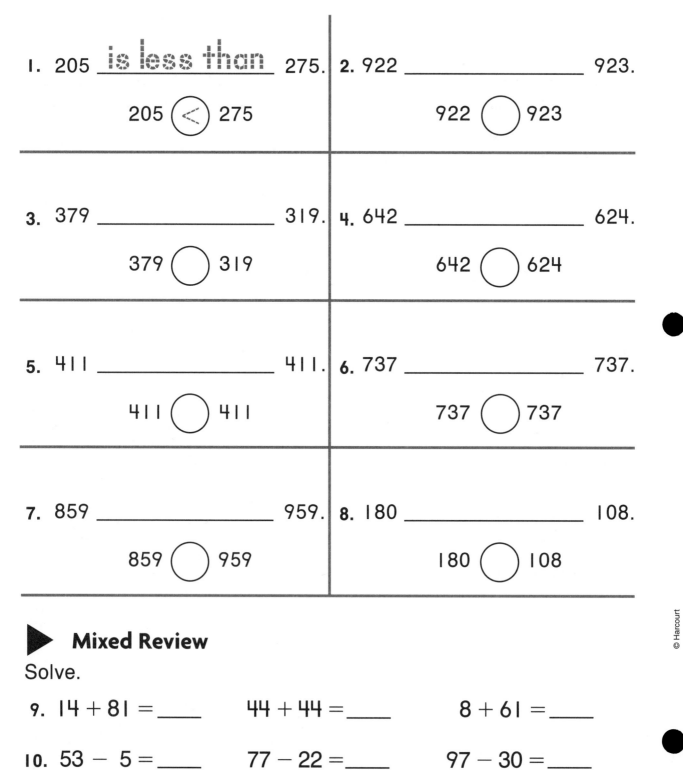

1. 205 __is less than__ 275.

205 ⟨<⟩ 275

2. 922 _____ 923.

922 ◯ 923

3. 379 _____ 319.

379 ◯ 319

4. 642 _____ 624.

642 ◯ 624

5. 411 _____ 411.

411 ◯ 411

6. 737 _____ 737.

737 ◯ 737

7. 859 _____ 959.

859 ◯ 959

8. 180 _____ 108.

180 ◯ 108

▶ **Mixed Review**

Solve.

9. $14 + 81 =$ ____ $44 + 44 =$ ____ $8 + 61 =$ ____

10. $53 - 5 =$ ____ $77 - 22 =$ ____ $97 - 30 =$ ____

Name _____

Missing Numbers to 1,000

Use 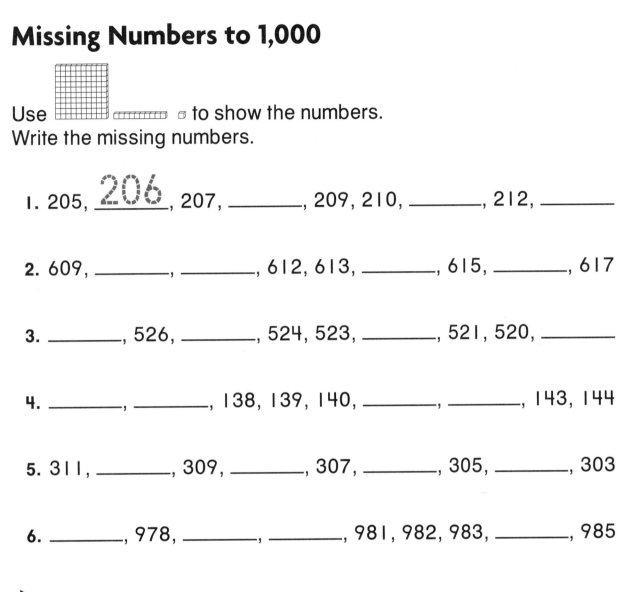 to show the numbers.
Write the missing numbers.

1. 205, __206__, 207, _____, 209, 210, _____, 212, _____

2. 609, _____, _____, 612, 613, _____, 615, _____, 617

3. _____, 526, _____, 524, 523, _____, 521, 520, _____

4. _____, _____, 138, 139, 140, _____, _____, 143, 144

5. 311, _____, 309, _____, 307, _____, 305, _____, 303

6. _____, 978, _____, _____, 981, 982, 983, _____, 985

▶ **Mixed Review**

Write the total amount.

7.
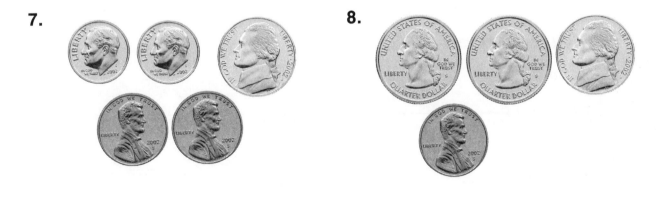

8.

_____   _____

© Harcourt

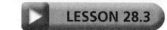

Algebra: Order Numbers on a Number Line

Write the numbers in order from least to greatest.
Use the number line to help you.

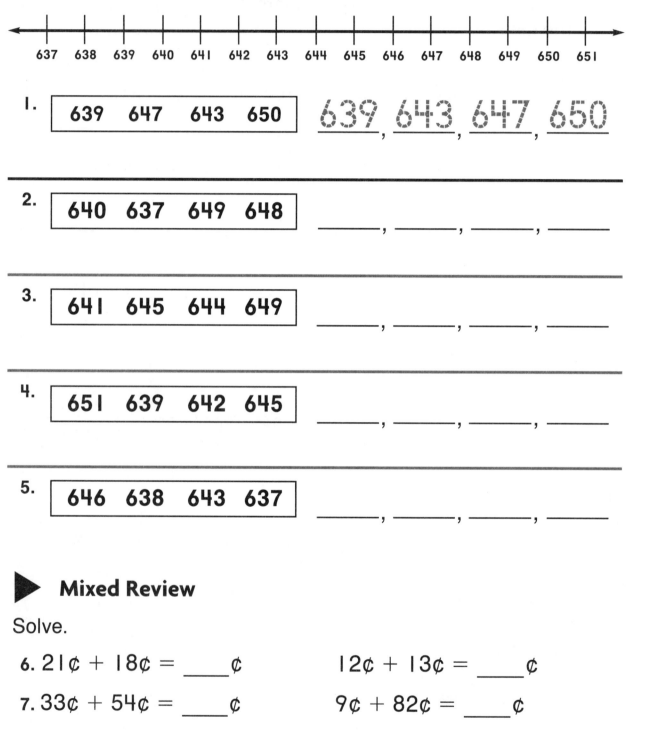

637 638 639 640 641 642 643 644 645 646 647 648 649 650 651

1. | 639 647 643 650 | 639, 643, 647, 650

2. | 640 637 649 648 | _____, _____, _____, _____

3. | 641 645 644 649 | _____, _____, _____, _____

4. | 651 639 642 645 | _____, _____, _____, _____

5. | 646 638 643 637 | _____, _____, _____, _____

▶ **Mixed Review**

Solve.

6. 21¢ + 18¢ = ____ ¢   12¢ + 13¢ = ____ ¢

7. 33¢ + 54¢ = ____ ¢   9¢ + 82¢ = ____ ¢

Name _____

Algebra: Find Unknown Numbers on a Number Line

Find A, B, and C on the number line.
Then write the number.

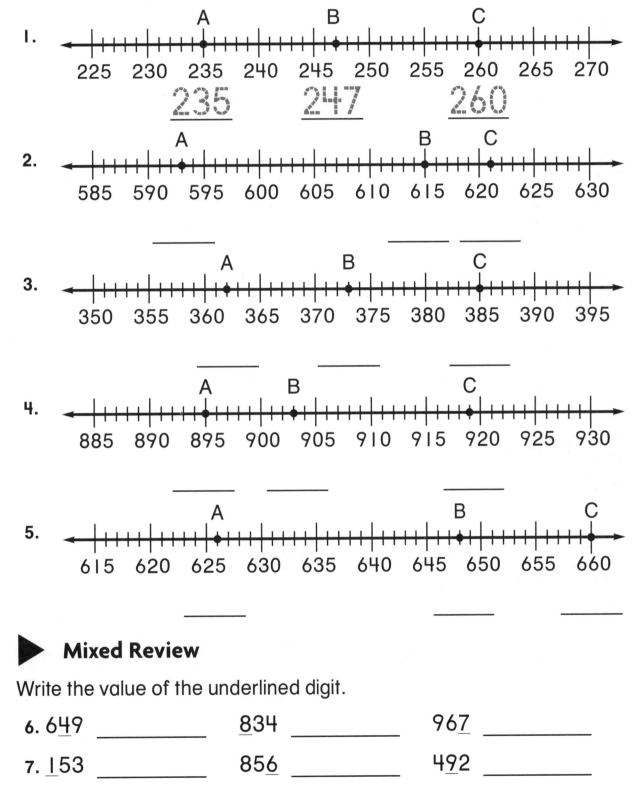

1. 235   247   260

Mixed Review

Write the value of the underlined digit.

6. 6<u>4</u>9 _____   <u>8</u>34 _____   96<u>7</u> _____

7. <u>1</u>53 _____   85<u>6</u> _____   4<u>9</u>2 _____

Algebra • Skip-Count

Skip-count. Write the missing numbers.

1. 243, 253, 263, _____, _____, _____, _____, 313

2. 785, 790, 795, _____, _____, _____, _____, 820

3. 651, 655, 659, _____, _____, _____, _____, 679

4. 122, 124, 126, _____, _____, _____, _____, 136

5. 504, 507, 510, _____, _____, _____, _____, 525

6. 400, 450, 500, _____, _____, _____, _____, 750

▶ Mixed Review

Subtract.

7.
$$\begin{array}{r} 39 \\ -18 \\ \hline \end{array} \quad \begin{array}{r} 63 \\ -24 \\ \hline \end{array} \quad \begin{array}{r} 42 \\ -35 \\ \hline \end{array} \quad \begin{array}{r} 53 \\ -28 \\ \hline \end{array} \quad \begin{array}{r} 77 \\ -40 \\ \hline \end{array}$$

8.
$$\begin{array}{r} 25 \\ -13 \\ \hline \end{array} \quad \begin{array}{r} 73 \\ -24 \\ \hline \end{array} \quad \begin{array}{r} 59 \\ -32 \\ \hline \end{array} \quad \begin{array}{r} 81 \\ -47 \\ \hline \end{array} \quad \begin{array}{r} 45 \\ -19 \\ \hline \end{array}$$

© Harcourt

Problem Solving • Find a Pattern

Write the pattern rule.
Write the next number in the pattern.

THINK: Look across the rows.

1.

401	402	403	404	405	406	407	408	409	410
411	412	413	414	415	416	417	418	419	420
421	422	423	424	425	426	427	428	429	430
431	432	433	434	435	436	437	438	439	440
441	442	443	444	445	446	447	448	449	450

Rule: _____

Next number: _____

2.

801	802	803	804	805	806	807	808	809	810
811	812	813	814	815	816	817	818	819	820
821	822	823	824	825	826	827	828	829	830
831	832	833	834	835	836	837	838	839	840
841	842	843	844	845	846	847	848	849	850

Rule: _____

Next number: _____

3.

101	102	103	104	105	106	107	108	109	110
111	112	113	114	115	116	117	118	119	120
121	122	123	124	125	126	127	128	129	130
131	132	133	134	135	136	137	138	139	140
141	142	143	144	145	146	147	148	149	150

Rule: _____

Next number: _____

Mental Math: Add Hundreds

Add. Write the number sentence.

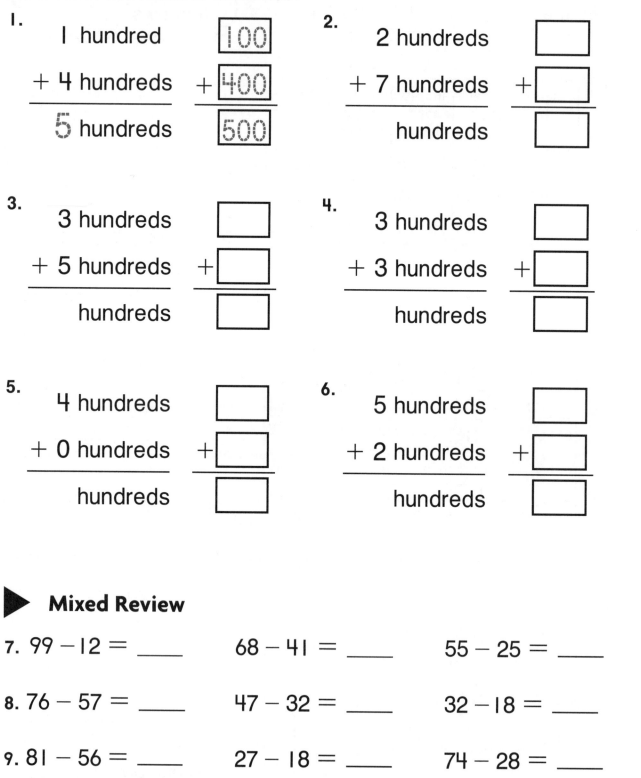

1.
1 hundred	100
+ 4 hundreds	+ 400
5 hundreds	500

2.
2 hundreds ☐
+ 7 hundreds + ☐
hundreds ☐

3.
3 hundreds ☐
+ 5 hundreds + ☐
hundreds ☐

4.
3 hundreds ☐
+ 3 hundreds + ☐
hundreds ☐

5.
4 hundreds ☐
+ 0 hundreds + ☐
hundreds ☐

6.
5 hundreds ☐
+ 2 hundreds + ☐
hundreds ☐

▶ **Mixed Review**

7. $99 - 12 = $ _____ $68 - 41 = $ _____ $55 - 25 = $ _____

8. $76 - 57 = $ _____ $47 - 32 = $ _____ $32 - 18 = $ _____

9. $81 - 56 = $ _____ $27 - 18 = $ _____ $74 - 28 = $ _____

Name _____

Model 3-Digit Addition: Regroup Ones

Use Workmat 5 and ▦ ▭ . Add.

1.
hundreds	tens	ones
	[1]	
2	3	9
+ 2	0	2
4	4	1

2.
hundreds	tens	ones
	[ ]	
8	0	6
+ 1	2	7

3.
hundreds	tens	ones
	[ ]	
1	2	9
+ 4	1	3

4.
hundreds	tens	ones
	[ ]	
2	3	6
+ 3	1	6

5.
hundreds	tens	ones
	[ ]	
8	0	7
+ 1	3	4

6.
hundreds	tens	ones
	[ ]	
6	2	8
+	1	3

7.
hundreds	tens	ones
	[ ]	
3	5	5
+ 2	1	8

8.
hundreds	tens	ones
	[ ]	
8	1	8
+	7	3

9.
hundreds	tens	ones
	[ ]	
5	4	7
+ 2	2	9

▶ **Mixed Review**

How many hundreds, tens, and ones are there?

10. 862 = ____ hundreds   ____ tens   ____ ones

11. 729 = ____ hundreds   ____ tens   ____ ones

12. 376 = ____ hundreds   ____ tens   ____ ones

Name _____

LESSON 29.3

Model 3-Digit Addition: Regroup Tens

Use Workmat 5 and [grid] [rod] [cube]. Add.

1.

hundreds	tens	ones
[1] 2	[1] 1	7
+ 1	9	9
4	1	6

2.

hundreds	tens	ones
[ ] 4	[ ] 2	9
+ 1	7	7

3.

hundreds	tens	ones
[ ] 2	[ ] 2	5
+ 5	8	6

4. 429
  + 187

5. 675
  + 153

6. 321
  + 296

7. 523
  + 406

8. 199
  + 730

9. 462
  + 450

10. 610
  + 198

11. 725
  + 92

▶ **Mixed Review**

Write the fraction for the shaded part.

12.

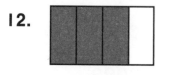 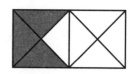

_____ _____ _____

© Harcourt

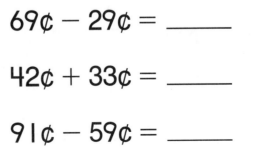
Mental Math: Subtract Hundreds

Subtract. Write the missing numbers.

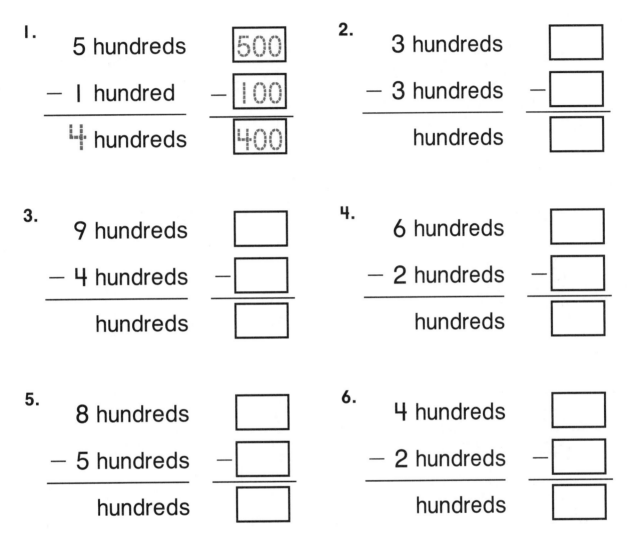

1.

    5 hundreds   500

− 1 hundred   − 100

4 hundreds   400

2.

    3 hundreds   [ ]

− 3 hundreds   − [ ]

hundreds   [ ]

3.

    9 hundreds   [ ]

− 4 hundreds   − [ ]

hundreds   [ ]

4.

    6 hundreds   [ ]

− 2 hundreds   − [ ]

hundreds   [ ]

5.

    8 hundreds   [ ]

− 5 hundreds   − [ ]

hundreds   [ ]

6.

    4 hundreds   [ ]

− 2 hundreds   − [ ]

hundreds   [ ]

▶ **Mixed Review**

Add or subtract.

7. 72¢ − 11¢ = _____   69¢ − 29¢ = _____

8. 55¢ + 37¢ = _____   42¢ + 33¢ = _____

9. 86¢ − 49¢ = _____   91¢ − 59¢ = _____

© Harcourt

Model 3-Digit Subtraction: Regroup Tens

Use Workmat 5 and 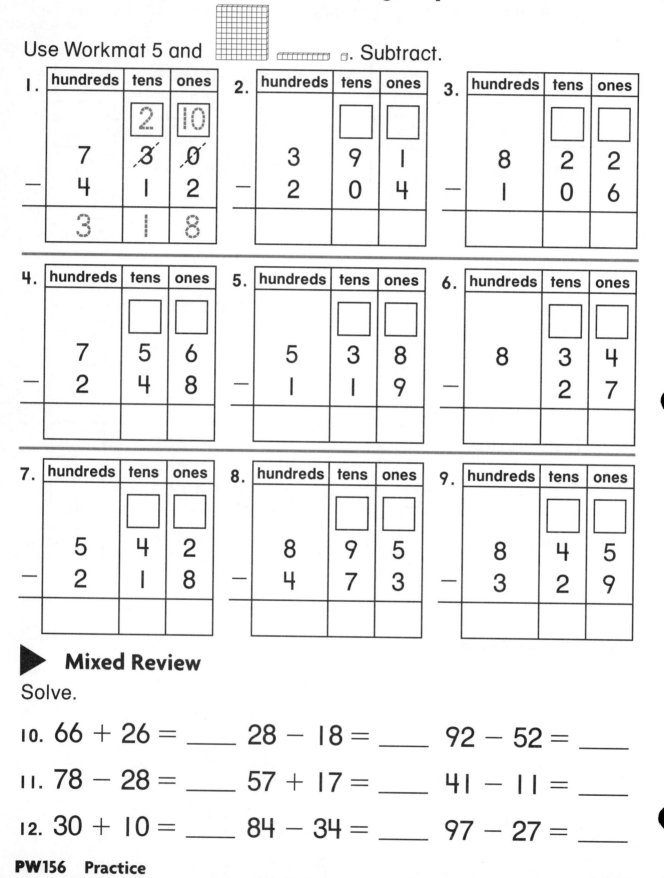 ▭ ⬚. Subtract.

1.

hundreds	tens	ones
	2	10
7	3̷	0̷
− 4	1	2
3	1	8

2.

hundreds	tens	ones
	☐	☐
3	9	1
− 2	0	4

3.

hundreds	tens	ones
	☐	☐
8	2	2
− 1	0	6

4.

hundreds	tens	ones
	☐	☐
7	5	6
− 2	4	8

5.

hundreds	tens	ones
	☐	☐
5	3	8
− 1	1	9

6.

hundreds	tens	ones
	☐	☐
8	3	4
−	2	7

7.

hundreds	tens	ones
	☐	☐
5	4	2
− 2	1	8

8.

hundreds	tens	ones
	☐	☐
8	9	5
− 4	7	3

9.

hundreds	tens	ones
	☐	☐
8	4	5
− 3	2	9

▶ **Mixed Review**

Solve.

10. $66 + 26 = $ _____ $28 - 18 = $ _____ $92 - 52 = $ _____

11. $78 - 28 = $ _____ $57 + 17 = $ _____ $41 - 11 = $ _____

12. $30 + 10 = $ _____ $84 - 34 = $ _____ $97 - 27 = $ _____

Name _____

Model 3-Digit Subtraction: Regroup Hundreds

Use Workmat 5 and 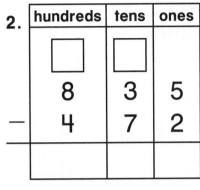 . Subtract.

1.	hundreds	tens	ones
	5̶ 6̶	1̶0̶ 0̶	6
−	2	5	2
	3	5	4

2.	hundreds	tens	ones
	☐ 8	☐ 3	5
−	4	7	2

3.	hundreds	tens	ones
	4	☐ 6	☐ 2
−		3	3

4.   504
   − 182

5.   824
   − 654

6.   229
   − 86

7.   682
   − 663

8.   303
   − 111

9.   924
   − 193

10.   543
    − 527

11.   685
    − 478

▶ **Mixed Review**

Write the number that is greater.

12. 916, 961 _____

13. 777, 727 _____

14. 227, 272 _____

15. 111, 191 _____

16. 585, 515 _____

17. 629, 692 _____

Problem Solving • Solve Multistep Problems

Add or subtract.

Do one step at a time.

	Step 1	Step 2
1. Peter saves $7.45. His sister gives him $2.37. He uses the money to buy a toy car for $6.81. How much money does Peter have left? <u>$3.01</u>	$7.45 +$2.37 $9.82	$9.82 −$6.81 $3.01
2. Maria has $3.25 in her piggy bank. She earns $2.50 doing chores. She spends $2.10. How much money does Maria have left? _____		
3. Wanda has $2.95. Her brother has $3.27. They need $8.15 to buy a present. How much more money do they need? _____		
4. Juanita buys a notebook for $1.99 and a box of crayons for $2.01. She gives the clerk $5.00. How much change does she get back? _____		

Addition and Multiplication

Write the sum. Then write the product.

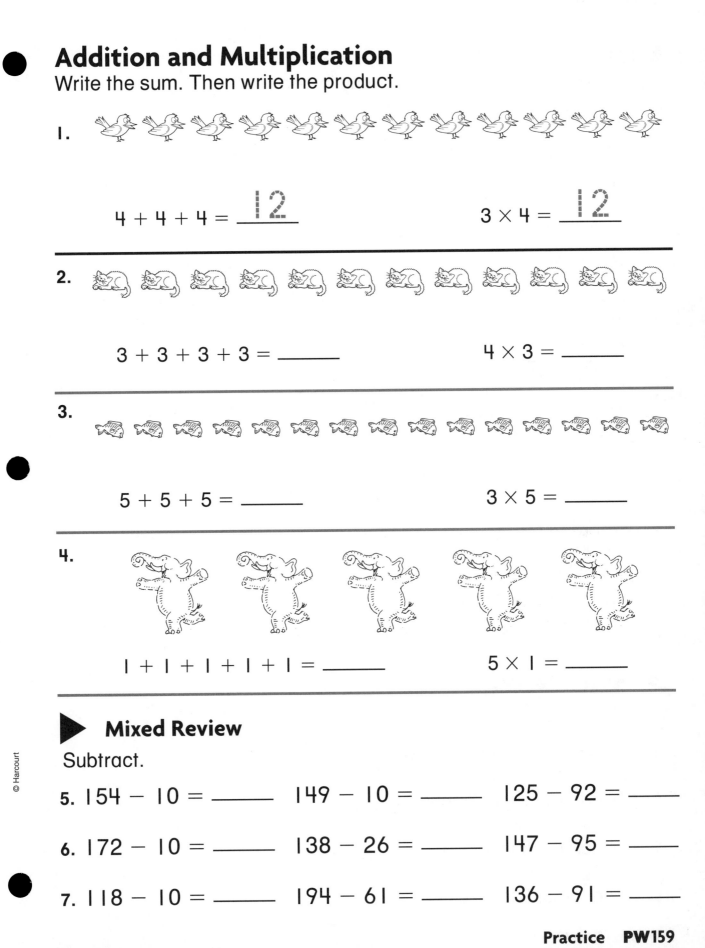

1.

$4 + 4 + 4 =$ __12__ $3 \times 4 =$ __12__

2.

$3 + 3 + 3 + 3 =$ _____ $4 \times 3 =$ _____

3.

$5 + 5 + 5 =$ _____ $3 \times 5 =$ _____

4.

$1 + 1 + 1 + 1 + 1 =$ _____ $5 \times 1 =$ _____

▶ **Mixed Review**

Subtract.

5. $154 - 10 =$ ____ $149 - 10 =$ ____ $125 - 92 =$ ____

6. $172 - 10 =$ ____ $138 - 26 =$ ____ $147 - 95 =$ ____

7. $118 - 10 =$ ____ $194 - 61 =$ ____ $136 - 91 =$ ____

Arrays

Write how many rows and how many in each row.
Write the product.

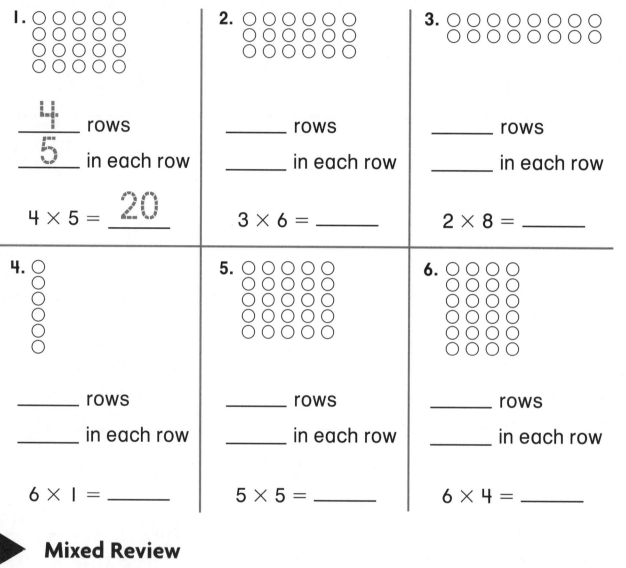

1. _____ rows

   _____ in each row

   $4 \times 5 =$ _____20_____

2. _____ rows

   _____ in each row

   $3 \times 6 =$ _____

3. _____ rows

   _____ in each row

   $2 \times 8 =$ _____

4. _____ rows

   _____ in each row

   $6 \times 1 =$ _____

5. _____ rows

   _____ in each row

   $5 \times 5 =$ _____

6. _____ rows

   _____ in each row

   $6 \times 4 =$ _____

▶ **Mixed Review**

Write the number.

7. 3 hundreds, 4 tens, 7 ones _____

8. 6 hundreds, 1 ten, 3 ones _____

9. 5 hundreds, 5 tens, 1 one _____

10. 8 hundreds, 3 tens, 2 ones _____

Name _____

Multiply in Any Order

Write the product.
Write the multiplication sentence in a different order.

1.

$4 \times 5 = \underline{20}$

$\underline{5} \times \underline{4} = \underline{20}$

2.

$10 \times 3 = \underline{}$

$\underline{} \times \underline{} = \underline{}$

3.

$2 \times 9 = \underline{}$

$\underline{} \times \underline{} = \underline{}$

4.

$3 \times 7 = \underline{}$

$\underline{} \times \underline{} = \underline{}$

5.

$6 \times 3 = \underline{}$

$\underline{} \times \underline{} = \underline{}$

6.

$8 \times 2 = \underline{}$

$\underline{} \times \underline{} = \underline{}$

7.

$7 \times 10 = \underline{}$

$\underline{} \times \underline{} = \underline{}$

8.

$3 \times 8 = \underline{}$

$\underline{} \times \underline{} = \underline{}$

▶ **Mixed Review**

Write the number that comes next. | Find the sum.

9. 10, 20, 30, 40, _____

10. 6, 12, 18, 24, _____

11. 3, 6, 9, 12, _____

12. $2+2+2+2+2+2+2 = \underline{}$

13. $5+5+5+5+5 = \underline{}$

14. $4+4+4+4+4+4 = \underline{}$

Practice PW161

Equal Groups: Size of Groups

Divide into equal groups. Some may be left over.
Draw to show. Write how many.

1. Divide 12 apples into 3 equal groups.

   ___4___ in each group

   ___0___ left over

2. Divide 9 oranges into 2 equal groups.

   _____ in each group

   _____ left over

3. Divide 16 pears into 3 equal groups.

   _____ in each group

   _____ left over

▶ **Mixed Review**

Count the parts. Write each fraction.
Write the fraction for the whole.

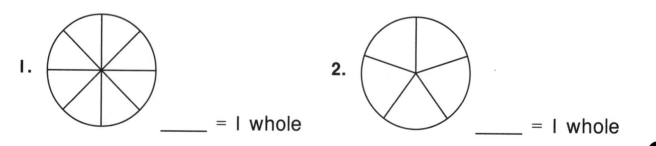

1. _____ = 1 whole

2. _____ = 1 whole

Equal Groups: Number of Groups

Circle equal groups.
Write how many groups there are.
Write how many are left over.

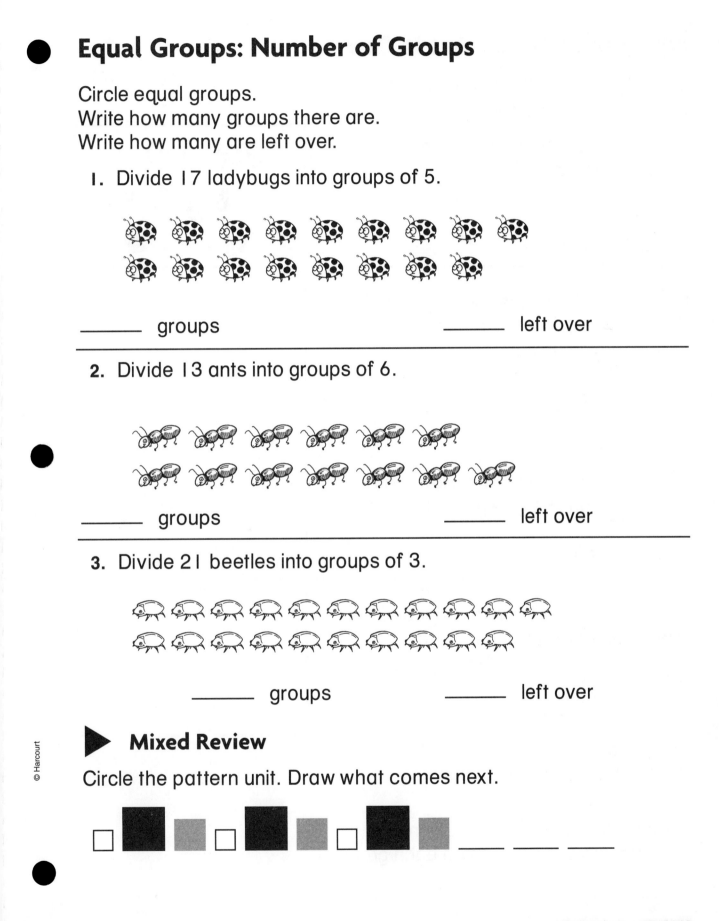

1. Divide 17 ladybugs into groups of 5.

_____ groups   _____ left over

2. Divide 13 ants into groups of 6.

_____ groups   _____ left over

3. Divide 21 beetles into groups of 3.

_____ groups   _____ left over

▶ **Mixed Review**

Circle the pattern unit. Draw what comes next.

© Harcourt

Problem Solving • Act It Out

Use counters to act out the problem.
Draw a picture to show your work.

1. LaToya has 12 marbles. She sorts them into 6 equal groups. How many marbles are in each group?

    __2__ marbles

2. Walt has 8 toy cars. He puts them into two equal rows. How many toy cars are in each row?

    _____ toy cars

3. Janell has 14 plums. She would like to give 2 to each friend. How many friends can she give plums to?

    _____ friends

4. There are 4 children at Amanda's house. Each child has 3 toys. How many toys are there in all?

    _____ toys

Create your own story.
Have a friend act it out to solve.

5. Antonio has _____.
   He puts them into _____ groups.
   How many _____ are in each group?

_____